STEERING BLIND

STEVE MARTELL *with*
REBECCA MAYGLOTHLING

Foreword by **DAN S. CARROLL**

Dedicated to everyone who has
touched my life, in particular
my wife Mari Grace.
God bless you all...*and keep rocking on!*

-Steve-

Steering Blind

Copyright © 2022 Steve Martell. *All rights reserved.*

ISBN 978-1-66786-896-7 (Print)

ISBN 978-1-66786-897-4 (eBook)

FOREWORD

I have known Steven Martell (Steve) for nearly fifty years. We met when we were 12 years old, in Junior High school. I was somewhat of an introvert back then, and Steve...*was not!* Far from it, in fact. He was a jokester, a talented musician, a pole-vaulter, and a very popular student.

We struck up a conversation about music one day and we've been great friends ever since. Steve had "street cred" in our rural school, and our friendship helped bring me out of my shell. He talked me into getting on stage, had me join the chorus, and even talked me into being the track and field announcer! I really think that last one was for his own personal entertainment, because clearly it wasn't the exact Wolfman Jack role I hoped for.

Steve has a great sense of humor that can lighten any mood. Many of the lessons he shares in Steering Blind are injected with his brand of humor, making this a very entertaining read. More importantly, this is a journey through the eyes of someone who had nearly everything taken from him, both physically and mentally, and found a way to be triumphant. Put simply, Steve chose life over death, and turned his personal tragedy into a never-ending commitment to help others with physical and mental challenges.

This book is an amusing jaunt through Steve's youth, the sudden nature of his accident, and his undying determination to create a new future for himself, and ultimately for others. For those who are disabled, this is undeniable proof that disabilities cannot defeat you if you remain determined and are willing to alter your path in life. This is a must read whether you are disabled or able bodied and has a great number of life lessons to draw from. In the simplest form, Steve teaches the reader to control their own outcomes in life, rather than letting obstacles control their future.

Steve's story is the epitome of leading by example.

I am proud to say that after a month in a coma, my friend Steve pulled up his bootstraps and got on with life. He worked very hard on his physical rehabilitation, leaving his wheelchair behind long after his doctors left him with little hope of that happening. He subsequently earned two master's degrees and has spent his entire professional life helping others with severe disabilities, most recently as Rehabilitation Counselor for the

Veterans Administration. This book, as well as his life, are full and rich, with faith, family, and friends; always filled with humor.

I hope you'll enjoy reading Steering Blind as much as I did. It's a very motivating and entertaining ride!

by Dan S. Carroll – Vice President, ABB, Inc. – Retired

CONTENTS

INTRODUCTION

On a muggy evening in 1969, I stood outside the bathroom door. I was listening for the shower water to turn off, and as soon as it did, I started knocking. I heard my dad pull back the shower curtain while I begged to come in. After about 30 seconds he belched loudly and said, "Okay."

I opened the door to see him in his Long John's; he was staring at the mirror over the sink. A bottle of Ballantine Ale rested on the edge. Months prior, Dad had built a small triangular shelf in the corner next to the mirror. On top of that, he constructed a mini cardboard pyramid that was hinged on top, kind of like opening a chest. There was a thread spool pedestal in the open structure with a shaving razor blade resting on it.

Dad told everyone the power of the Egyptian pyramids channeled through the replica and kept the blade sharp. He said the blade had to be angled exactly right to grab the magic rays from Egypt. I was just a seven-year-old kid. I thought Egypt was the next town over, so I believed him. However, he always came out of the bathroom with wads of toilet paper stuck all over his face, so I figured he had to adjust the angle of the blade slightly.

My brother Dave told me once he saw Dad pull a piece of shrapnel from his face when shaving, and I was dying to see that happen. That's what attracted me to study his shaving. I could care less about the pyramid. He would swipe down his face, rinse, repeat. Sometimes he'd take a swig of beer between swipes.

This was my life back then. Laid back and full of silly beliefs that probably were not true. But, hey, maybe they are true? In any event, my growing years where simple and fun... that was until tragedy came. Yeah, life hit me pretty dang hard and almost knocked the fun out of me in my late teen years. I spent a lot of time wondering if I'd ever regain my happiness. But you know, there came a time when I decided I was going to find the fun in life again, *and I got it back!* I took that smack in the face from life and I threw it back in life's face. I came back to the playful, carefree kid in me and have focused on helping other people ever since. I aim to help people with disabilities crawl from the same dungeon I was in and come back to the fun!

I wrote this book because I want to share my story with others. I don't do it to show off or tell others what to do; I do it because I see a real need in the world. I see others who need help like I did, and I want them to know this support exists. Many people don't know they can take ownership of their lives or how they can find the right public programs. Here's some news for you all: *I do know,* and through the school of hard knocks. Furthermore, don't think these programs are government "hand-me-outs", not by any means, because YOU can become society's return! Hey, I've been through the trenches of rehabilitation for people with disabilities and I'd love to show you how it's done.

But to capitalize on recovery you must be willing to stop comparing yourself to able-bodied people or how you were before your disability. Maximize what you have and massage it, and don't dwell on doing the impossible. Say, I'd like to flap my arms and fly to a second story on a building. I could waste my life flapping away but still not move. Instead, I get things done on ground level and take the elevator to the second floor if I must. Now, apply that concept to having a disability.

I want to share my story with you to give you encouragement. I want you to see me and see my life, as my life is your life. I want you to get to know me so you will feel like you can do your variation of what I've done. I want you to know you can do it and most importantly, *believe in yourself.* Not only do I want to help you find programs that can benefit you, but I'm going to hit your funny bone! For those of you who grew up in the 70's, like me, I'll give you a bit of nostalgia. It'll be fun. For anyone else, I'll give you a bit of history. It'll be fascinating. But what I'll give you most of all is hope, and resources to help you in your life while giving respect to your disability.

Keep reading. Let's go back to a simpler time before the Internet. Let's all talk about what that was like and let's share laughs before we get into the real tragedy of my life, then move on to how I found new hope. Come with me and check out the answers I can give you. At the end, you might say, "Hey, thanks Steve," or you might say, "Meh. This doesn't work at all." Whatever way you go with my book, thanks for giving me a chance. But most of all, after you read this book, I hope you give yourself a chance.

CHAPTER I

THE EARLY YEARS

I was born on Flag Day in 1962 in the *real* Upstate New York. I was closer to Canada than I was to New Jersey; it was all lakes and country living. You wouldn't find skyscrapers within 250 miles of my house. Strange as it seems, some of my best memories involve mud and lakes.

Life was easy.

My family was carefree and always had something going on. Our house was full of people all the time, so I guess you could say being lonely wasn't an option. When your parents have eight kids, you get a full house even when no one's over to visit.

I was the youngest of those eight. My brother Mike was the oldest, followed by Patt, Rick, Diane, and Don, who were twins, Dave, and Jeanmarie. My father had nicknames for all of us and mine was "Hunkey" because he said I was born with fuzzy blonde hair. I still can't figure out the connection. All I know is some people never knew my real name until I was thirteen.

It was the wonder years for me, growing up in our country setting just outside Syracuse, New York - simple life, simple times. It was my entire family who truly inspired and shaped me.

Us kids had a normal childhood. The term "normal" is used loosely here; what was normal back then is anything but normal today. We believed things that were blatant lies because there was no Google to go ask or Siri to echo back. We got really bored sometimes because we didn't have constant entertainment at our fingertips, but the boredom made the fun times all the better.

When I say it was simple times with clean fun, I mean it! We found things to do for entertainment, and those things weren't always in our best interest. What did we know, though? Our parents let us have the run of the neighborhood because a "helicopter" was still something that flew around in the sky, not a parent who looked over our shoulder every second. Everyone trusted everyone else. Girl Scouts could actually knock-on doors to sell cookies, not count on their parents to sell them in their work breakrooms. My brother Rick could nonchalantly speed down our road with his Go-Kart, usually with a spotter to heed warning of oncoming traffic. Yeah, growing up was different back then. I don't know if it was safer, but it sure was different.

Our house wasn't anything fancy, but it was comfortable enough. For some reason, my mom was always trying to hide it from passing traffic. We had three swamp willows in the front yard that always had giant puddles under them, as well as a few large lilac bushes, which suited Mom just fine. Those puddles rarely went away and are a big part of my childhood.

Always on Black Friday, Mom would have us kids cut down a large pine tree from our forest out back and put the trunk in one of the puddles. There it would stay for two weeks until we dragged it inside for Christmas. I'd always try to help decorate the tree with my sisters, and Jeanmarie would always get mad at me for heaping the tinsel on the lower branches. To my sister's relief, soon I would lose interest and fall back to watching *Rudolph* or *The Grinch*.

We had a normal looking house - a long ranch house that my father built around 1960. When you walked in the front door, there was a long dining room table in a room that was supposed to be a living room. It had two leaves that would extend its length for special holidays such as Thanksgiving and Christmas, and that was our "special events" area. Every

Christmas, we would call my grandparents in frigid Old Forge, New York, and every year, Grandpa Martell would convince us that he was helping Santa grease the runners on the sleigh. That holiday table was as much a part of the holidays as that annual phone call.

To the left was a sliding wooden door that opened to a kitchen, that usually came off its rolling track. The kitchen also had a big table that wasn't as nice as the special events number in the living room. It was that funky 70's chrome and yellow style that's only found in 50's themed restaurants today. The living room was sunk into the floor in the style of the times and had an old black and white TV. We used to have to "warm it up" to get an image to gradually show and it only had four stations: CBS, ABC, NBC, and Public Broadcasting. Dad loved Ed Sullivan. In fact, when Dad cooked for us, he'd watch Ed and assign one of us to give the set a few good whacks when the picture started to roll. I watched Quinn-Martin Productions, Hee Haw, Smother's Brothers, Hogan's Heroes, Laugh-in, Green Acres, Columbo, and MASH. I stayed away from Lawrence Welk, but my parents liked it. I was all boy, and my TV was all humor, with a few Clint Eastwood movies for flavor. "Go ahead punk, make my day," was my favorite catch phrase.

The TV stations would go off at midnight to the National Anthem and come back on at 6 am. During that off time there would be nothing but a fuzzy looking screen called a "snow screen".

There were antennas on the roof that captured the signal directly from the station, and sometimes, the stations would fail. A screen on a failed station would pop up that said, "Please stand by." My brother Dave would tell me to go stand next to the television when this happened, and I did it because I thought that's what we had to do. He said the electric aura of everyone standing by their sets would charge up the station and bring the picture back. What did I know?

Scattered around the house were five bedrooms with an extra big one for my parents. One wall in my parent's room was almost all closets. They slept in separate beds, and I snoozed in a 60's style crib in their room until I was five. We had a full bath with a separate shower and a showerhead over the bathtub. I never understood why we had two showers in one room. Maybe to rinse off multiple muddy kids at one time?

To the right of the tub was the sink with Dad's magical blade sharpening pyramid overhead. There was a half bath outside the kitchen - a real blessing with so many people. I can't imagine one bathroom in a house that full! The smell of Lucky Strike cigarettes will always remind me of home due to Mom and Dad smoking them indoors for years. There was a shelf in the refrigerator dedicated to school lunches, and I remember watching Mom line up bread for sandwiches. My mother was amazing; she could whip out sandwiches on a one-person assembly line like nobody's business!

There was a three-car wide driveway made from stone, dirt, and several mud puddles with a garage door on both ends. I think Dad intended on finishing the driveway in a circular pattern so we could drive through the garage, but that never happened, so it remained a mosaic of crushed stone and dirt.

There was no sewer or plumbing in the area, but there were many underground springs around. My Aunt Joan came over with her gift for finding water. She used a peach branch in the shape of a "Y" for what she called "dowsing." She showed Dad where to dig and he hit a bubbly "geyser". We used that for water in the house. I'll never forget the smell of the sulfur water that supported our family all those years. I always came out of the tub smelling like a rotten egg and I think I smelled better caked in mud. But seeing how my aunt located a thin vein and no spring, our well would dry up in the summer so we would go to the local gas station with empty milk bottles. Back then, the gas stations had free community hoses, so we filled the bottles up and brought them home.

There was a laundry room in a musty basement. Mom would do the wash and scream occasionally over a salamander slithering across the floor. The basement wasn't finished, and the critters liked the dark dampness of it. Unfortunately, Mom would suffer the consequences. There were no gutters on the roof's edge, so the rain would seep into the cellar. I'm sure this didn't help Mom avoid the salamanders, but we had a good time with it! It's just one of those "unsung songs" I remember specifically about our house.

We always had dinner together as a family. My mother would make a big pot of something, like pasta with meat sauce, which we called goulash, but always in bulk. We weren't allowed to have the TV on or answer the phone during dinner. Sometimes, Dad would hide a candy bar in the kitchen, then while we ate, he would set one of us up to find it, but only if we said the "magic number."

He would say, "Hunkey, how many fingers do I have?"

I would say sarcastically, "Ah, five?"

His answer: "That's the lucky number! Go get the paper!"

Well, after I'd run round trip to the paper box, I'd either come back to a Mars Bar or an "IOU." Yes, it was a crapshoot, but it always had an element of excitement!

At times, Dad would cook up venison on the stove, gulping beer and watching TV. Occasionally, he'd add a swish of beer to the pan. Our dog would sit at his feet, waiting for fat or grizzle from the pan.

This was his Saturday. On other Saturdays, especially in the summer, we would have grilled burgers in the backyard. Dad would instruct me to point a blow torch at a piece of charcoal until it lit the grill, which took forever, as he detested lighter fluid. A real treat was having actual buns and not just sliced bread to go with our burgers. Sauteed mushrooms and onions on our patties seemed to be a holiday.

Relaxation for me was the creek (pronounced "crick") behind our house. We put down logs to walk over it and caught huge crayfish and bullfrogs. In the spring, a giant snapping turtle would lay eggs back there, and the hatchlings would parade across our yard. It was "The March of the Turtles," according to my mother. The mother turtles - *whoo!* - were nothing to mess with (just ask the guy who lost the tip of his finger teasing one), but the babies were usually harmless.

Don't ask me why, but once I put a baby turtle and a crayfish in a coffee can to see who would win in a fight, but they ignored each other. I was disappointed, but I figured that God wanted them to live in harmony, so I let them go free. Without knowing it, I learned that differences can make a relationship, though the lesson meant nothing to me at the time. I did learn quick not to mess with things with claws too often, though. I fell in the creek once and came up with a crawfish firmly holding the end of my nose, as my face landed in my bucket of crabs.

I used to pluck out nightcrawlers, which are large worms, on warm, damp nights, and even started a business with the neighbor. People *loved* nightcrawlers for catching fish, so a couple kids selling them for a few pennies was fine. Of course, we soon lost interest in all the hard work involved and abandoned

the idea. Besides, I needed the bait for my own fishing outings
and Dave said the IRS would come after me because I'm not
claiming the income on my taxes.

We used to ride our bikes down the street and build ramps,
and I thought I was Evil Knievel. I tried a big jump once, but the
chain on my bike snagged, and instead of making this awesome
jump in front of everyone, I bit it in the pavement. My scraped
knees told the story.

When I wasn't arranging wrestling fights between species
and trying to fly, I was picking strawberries for my cereal with
Theresa, the neighborhood tomboy. Wild strawberries grew
everywhere around us, but they weren't the same as the berries
in the store. They were much smaller, and 25 or so were enough
for a bowl of Rice Krispies.

Simple times, simple fun.

I guess you can say I was born into an atmosphere that
took pride in good, old fashioned 9-to-5 work. My father was
a foreman of an electronics company and would bust his butt
to provide for us. Again, I wanted to be like the old man, so at
the fresh age of 9 I started my job search. But I was lost; I just
couldn't find a good career path.

I recall one misty winter morning I was sitting at my
kitchen table, misspelling the word "failure" in my alphabet
cereal, when I heard a muffled voice yell outside, "Meter Man!"

This startled me. I was puzzled. I scurried from the kitchen table and peeked out the window, where I was greeted by some man in a blue coat and earmuffs, carrying a clipboard. He waded through the snow around our house, so I ran to the side window. Peering through a frosted pane, I watched as the man looked at the spinning top on our house's side and scribbled something down on his clipboard. Then fast as he came, he followed the snow trail he just blazed, climbed into a white car, and sped down the road into the foggy haze.

I looked at Mom and Dad in amazement, but they didn't seem to mind. Dad just kept on reading his magazine and Mom kept knitting her potholder. Our dog didn't even bark!

Needless to say, I was in total awe. I finally knew why God sent me to this earth: to look at spinning globes on the side of houses. The idea of marching into someone's yard like a soldier seemed so macho to me, so carefree. No one really knew what it was or what it did, but that didn't matter to me. I just fell in love with the low, commanding, authoritative yell bellowing out, "Meter Man!"

I decided to take action. I got ahold of a Meter Man poster. Dave sold me some Meter Man bubblegum cards, one who resembled Yogi Berra with a black wig. I started a "God, Save the Meter Man" campaign. I even made friends with a Meter Man who used to let me carry his Meter Man clipboard!

Well, I think my father got sick and tired always hearing about my Meter Man obsession. He called me over to his side one day, put his arm around my back, and said, "Hunkey, you're too short to be a Meter Man." I cried for three days and refused to take out the garbage for a week.

-And so, my job search continued-

I always had an AM transistor radio with me back then. If anyone remembers these things, they were small and bulky, but I didn't mind lugging it around. It became a part of me. I wondered if I could turn this state-of-the-art technology into a career. I loved bad weather, especially if it was a snow day from school. So, I thought about being a weatherman, and learned the scientific name was "meteorologist". Now THAT was a cool job title!

It was important for me to always be on top of the weather conditions. The report would play on my radio every hour and I would do my best to memorize it. Everyone knew this was my passion, so people would come find me for the weather report. Whenever anyone said, "Hey Hunkey, what's the weather like?" I'd slide into my memorized version:

"The weather? Well, funny you ask! After a cool, clammy day yesterday, you can expect plenty of sunshine today, with a high of 65 and a low of 48. Winds shifting from the west to southwest 5 to 10 miles per hour. If you're out on the water today, expect partly sunny skies with winds at 10 knots per hour. I can't rule out a stray shower coming off Lake Ontario."

Folks actually relied on me for the forecast; I thought that was wild! Today, I know those people liked the reports to plan out their day, but back then I had a hidden agenda: I just saw them as lab rats to practice being a meteorologist.

Then my sister Diane told me you have to go to college for six years to be a meteorologist, so I tabled that idea. *You're kidding?* I thought. *What kind of fool is gonna waste six years of their life behind a book?* Well, my career search soon lost steam and I decided to be a kid again.

Oddly enough, what sticks in my mind most growing up was noise, both inside and outside our house. You couldn't get around it, and it seemed to come in from all angles in every form.

In the 60's, my older brothers created a band called Mama's Boys. My father must have thought they'd be the next Jackson 5, because he bought a rusty old VW Transporter van to move their equipment. They loved the Beatles, just like everyone else in the world. In 1969, the Beatles performed an impromptu concert on the roof of their record company. It looked so cool, so my brothers wanted to copy it with a gig on top of our house. Well, my mother forbade them doing a "surprise concert" on the roof, so they settled for a pop-up gig on Oneida River at my grandparent's camp. Boaters would idle their crafts in the water to see the cute kids playing music and singing lyrics like, "Yummy-yummy" or covering Freddy and the Dreamers, "I'm Telling You Now," less the leg flanks.

During the day, you could hear Rick pounding the drums. He set the precedent for Dave and me, who were the future drummers of the house. By the time I was playing, though, my mother had been worn out. She tolerated Rick and Dave to an extent, but I had to get special permission to practice. Shouts of "Stop that damn pounding!" weren't foreign to me.

I felt bigger than life because I thought I was related to rock stars! They even let me plug in some cords from their Vox amps. Fancy that, I was a rock star's roadie. As I started to grow in the 70's I became interested in girls, and I realized their band was a girl magnet. Girls would come out in droves to see my brothers play. That sold it - *I needed to get into a band!*

"Someday," I told myself. "Someday."

My sister Jeanmarie played the clarinet, always walking the scale and cracking on the fifth note. It got to be a tradition; she would hit that distant blast after dinner almost every evening. Dave used to squint his eyes and said it sounded like the soundtrack of a Godzilla movie. But after a while she mastered that note. You would *never* see me near a clarinet, however. I thought playing one was *far* too girly for me and ignored it, so I focused on drums. There was a piano in the sunken living room. No one played it, besides someone plucking a few keys occasionally, but it was a contributor to our overall chaos.

In the late 70's, Rick bought a dirt modified racecar from a guy in a nearby town and turned our garage into a workshop. The car was good old 181. I can still hear the echo of the motor revving up in the garage, with a fan pumping carbon monoxide out the window. I was privileged when I got to go in the pits with him at the racetracks. Yeah, my brothers helped mold me and I spent my early years fixated on all things "manly".

My brother Mike, the oldest, especially had a huge impact on me, but I wouldn't know it until later in life. He was born with a learning disability. Around 1953 the doctors labeled him a "high class moron" and the diagnosis devastated my mother. He would never learn to read due to severe dyslexia. If he had been diagnosed today, people would have worked with him and tried to help him succeed. Back then, they simply gave him a label and sent him on his way. He wasn't allowed to participate in "normal" high school activities, but instead was forced to attend special education and play Donkey Basketball.

However, Mike persevered and got a job as a custodian at the school he attended. My mother said that, if he could read, he would have become a manager. Mothers know things about their kids; my mother saw Mike's work ethic and knew if he weren't enslaved with a developmental disability accompanied with a damning diagnosis, he could have moved mountains.

I adored my big brother and always got along with him. His disability never really bothered me. I always thought, "Yeah, that's Mike. That's how he is." Even when people around me were picking on people with a disability, I never really saw Mike as handicapped. Without trying, he set up my first image of people with a disability and how they are like the rest of us: simply people trying to make it in life.

Well, Mike did make it in life despite the demoralizing doctor's labels. Looking back, I'm sure he inspired me to do better in my own life, and I know we shared the same tenacity. He may have been trying to tell everyone something with how he plugged forward against adversity, but I never understood his message. Now I know what he tried to say to everyone. Still, when growing up, I saw myself as "invincible." I could *never* and would *never* become disabled! Actually, the thought never even came to my mind. The word "disabled" was just not in my vocabulary.

If you have read this far, you probably realize I was always in competition with my brother Dave. He probably never realized it and won't know it until he reads this book! He was the next oldest boy to me, and I wanted to do everything he did. In swim class, Dave was allowed to graduate to level six swimming, which meant he got to use the diving board. I never made it past level three, which was water up to my waist. I begged the swim instructor to let me move up like Dave and wound up with a nose full of chlorine. I quit swim lessons the same day.

Dave didn't typically try to outdo me; he was just older and wasn't Mom's baby like I was. He actually did help me grow, albeit in an unconventional way, like teaching me to ride a bike. Dave would gently usher me down a hill in the front yard. Then when no one was looking, he would let the bike go saying, "Sayonara!" and wave. We didn't have training wheels, so I had to either balance or land in a swamp willow puddle. Yes, our competition was something I dreamt up, because he was only four years older than me, and I felt entitled to the same liberties he had. Mom would let him drive his bike anywhere he wanted, but not me - I had to be escorted!

One summer day, my best friend Norm Mattice called me and said he was about to launch a plastic rocket that resembled Apollo 11. He was a model rocket enthusiast.

"Groovy!" I exclaimed. "I'll be right over."

I hung up the phone and took three last chugs of my Yoohoo, crushing the can on my knee and tossing it in the garbage. I walked up to my mother.

"Mom," I said to her, as she stirred tomato sauce on the stove, "can I go to Norm's house? He's gonna launch Apollo 11!" She rolled her eyes.

She said while not looking up from her sauce, "No, your Aunt Joan is coming over in a bit to show us photos of her trip to Italy. "

I pouted, "C'mon Mom, I can quickly ride my bike there and be back in two hours to look at the pictures."

"You're NOT going to ride your bike over there!" she said sternly.

"Why not? You let Dave ride his bike to Bill Dudley's house!"

"Your brother is also older than you" she said, now adding tomato paste to her sauce. "No, absolutely not."

In a fit of rage, I blurted out, "Well then, *screw you!*"

"*Joe!*" my mother yelled nonchalantly, while pressing more garlic in her pot.

"HUNKEY!!" I heard my father yell.

I scrunched my eyes together, not knowing he was in ear shot. I slowly opened them up, "Yeah?"

"GET YOUR ASS IN THE BEDROOM...*NOW!*"

My panic alarm rang four times. My father *never* yelled at me to "get in the bedroom" before, but he had Dave in there several times. I never knew what went on in there, but Dave always left with weepy eyes and sniffles.

My father stood in the threshold of the bedroom and held the door open. I walked slowly through it, head held low, like it was my last steps to a noose. The sound of the door slamming behind me jolted my spine.

At the same time thoughts were racing through my head: *how would I get out of this one? Could I convince Dad she heard me wrong?* It was my first major offence, so perhaps he would let me off with a warning.

I looked at my father with pathetic eyes and quickly fired out words, not skipping a beat: "Dad, I'm sorry! I must have lost my head! I should have never, EVER have said that! Please-please-please have mercy on my soul!" I dropped my face in my hands and started weeping. I was partly trying to make light of the situation and partly serious.

My father put his right hand on my shoulder, and I looked up to him with glassy eyes. He held a stern expression.

"Hunkey," he said to me, "your mother is going to want me to spank you, you know that, right?" I gulped hard. He continued, "But, I really don't want to."

I smiled, "Yeah?"

"We got to make it look good though," he said. "I tell you what. I'm going to take off my belt and start whipping the bed. Every time I hit it; I want you to yell like I hit you. Your mother will hear it and think I'm spanking you."

I smiled and pointed at him, "And mom will be happy with you, and I get a free pass. Great idea Dad!" I snickered, "Mom will never know the difference."

My father nodded and slowly took off his belt. He doubled it up and leaned towards the bed, "You ready?"

I grinned: "Ready."

Just before my father was going to hit the bed with his belt, he said, "Ah, you know, your mother may poke her head in the bedroom and see I'm hitting the bed." He looked both ways and said in a hushed tone, "I tell you what Hunk, why don't you slump over the bed, just to make it look good?"

"Okay Dad," I said. I leaned over the bed with my rear-end sticking out.

"Hey Hunkey, why don't you pull down your trousers, so your mother could see your underwear? Just for effect."

I gleefully smiled and yanked my shorts down, "How's this Dad?" I made a muffled chuckle with my face plastered in the bed, "Boy, this is gonna be great!"

"You bet your sweet ass it is," he said. Then...

WHAP!

He whipped me square on the rear.

"AHHGGGG!!" I screamed, startled. I raised my head up while he forced his knee on my legs, pinning me to the bed.

"You're doing a great job!" my father exclaimed.

WHAP!

"ARRGGG!!"

"Keep it up! You're so convincing!"

WHAP!

"STOPP!! I'M SORRY!!"

"What did you say to your mother?"

WHAP!

At that point, I got out from under my father's knee, tripped on my pant legs, slammed my head on the door, spun the knob around, then flopped out in the hallway.

That was the first—and last time—I ever swore at my parents.

• • •

Other things I remember about where we lived was the sometimes crazy weather we would get, like the big blizzard of 1966. This storm dropped about 60 inches of snow on us over four days and blasted us with some of the coldest weather ever felt in Upstate New York. We got lake effect snow all the time, but this was the monster of all snowstorms. The snow hit the ground and the wind whipped it against the house. The windows were covered and inside it was eerily dim. The little daylight that could get in was paled by the massive piles of snow falling from the sky.

We all hunkered down indoors for the worst of it but couldn't wait to get outside! When we finally got out, my older siblings tobogganed off the roof into the drifts and drove snowmobiles to the Big M grocery store for milk.

Snowstorms were too common from late October to early May, and we tried to make the best of it, until the "snirt" season came and we were sick of it (snow *plus* dirt equals "snirt"). Every late winter, our boredom with snirt mounted so high, we would do crazy things, like tie a willing "victim" to the back of a snowmobile, with or without a sled, and take off. Once Norm became a victim and decided to use his snorkel jacket as a sled. All went fine, until the snowmobile ran over pavement. Norm tried to convince his mother his singed jacket was because of aggressive moths. He insisted they were so hungry last year they ate right through his buttons!

Simple times, simple fun.

Blizzards weren't the only time we had winter fun, though. We were kids whose parents weren't constantly carting us off to the next big adventure, so we had to find our own fun. When Norm and I were snowed in during the winter, we used the old rotary phone as a source of entertainment. We would drag out the phone book, find a victim's phone number randomly, and call them. No caller ID meant barely any chance of being caught. These crank calls were usually making animal noises into the phone, engaging in meaningless conversation, or asking for fictitious people. There was nothing clever or unique about them.

Once, Norm and I decided to overtake the phonebook when his parents were out. He told me his fingers walked over the yellow pages and started dancing on the white ones.

We found someone with a last name we didn't like. Norm dialed the number on the phone, and I sat in front of him with my shirt off; my left hand was cupped under my right armpit. He listened for someone to answer and when they did, he held the phone by my armpit, which was my cue to start pumping my arm, creating "farting sounds". He complemented my actions with "relief" utterances in the mouthpiece.

Again, these calls were very juvenile and immature, but we just got a kick out of the other person's reaction. It was the perfect storm to combat boredom!

To this day, I have my own version of "crank calls", except now, the people call me. Have you been told your car warranty is about to expire? You hang up, right? **Not me**

• • •

When warmer weather rolled around and we weren't tied to a phone, we would spend a lot of time outdoors, sometimes at my grandparents' camp on Oneida River. I remember trying to fish while Mike did cannonballs off the dock. I would get so mad because his big splashes scared the fish away, leaving nothing but a tidal wave of seaweed.

When I wanted to swim, my parents would tie a rope around my waist and tie the other end to the dock so I couldn't float away too far. I would doggy paddle until I was old enough to swim out further, and even though I quit swim classes, eventually I figured it out. For a long time, I was afraid to go out more than three yards because Dad said the eels would suck my blood if I did. It was a long time before I learned that most animals are more afraid of me than I am of them, but back then, that's how adults talked to kids. We all just went along with it.

Boats would chug down the river all summer and all my close relations would show up at our family camp. One year, we had a water balloon fight with my cousins, but my great aunt, the neat freak that she was, put an end to that quickly. She didn't want balloon pieces all over the yard and complained the birds would eat them.

When not at the camp, I remember shooting mice with my .22 rifle from the back of our house on rainy days. Field mice were all over the place outside, and guns were a natural part of growing up for many of us in Central New York. In fact, Dad had an old knee mortar gun in the corner of our living room, and there was a rifle club at school.

If you were in the Rifle Club in school, you got a special long locker to hold your weapon during classes. It was common to see the Rifle Club members walking to their after-school meetings with the rifle bags on their backs. The bullets were kept separate from the guns, and the members weren't allowed to have bullets outside of the place where they had their meetings. The point is guns were everywhere in school while mass shootings were not. I guess bad kids would not shoot good kids because they knew the good kids would shoot back. Yeah, it was a different time.

Our family was Catholic, and I went along with the religion, but didn't always practice it correctly. For instance, I always thought you had communion on Sunday to wipe out the sins of the week, but a few sins would still make it through. Kind of like a disinfectant that kills 99% of germs, but 1% remain. So, we all had confession once a year to kill that 1% of pesky sins that accumulated. I often wondered if you could see sin through a microscope.

I always gave the illusion of a kid with a halo around his head, so I would go to all Catholic gatherings, including those special religious education classes. In grade school and in middle school, all the Catholic kids could leave class once every two weeks to march across muddy fields to the rectory. One of our classmates, Tod Greenstein, told the teachers his name was O'Greenstein so he could get out of school early with the rest of us. Surprisingly, it worked for a few weeks! I don't know who finally caught on-maybe his yarmulke was the red flag-but his trick finally stopped. I remember seeing him pouting in class while the rest of us left.

Simple times, simple fun.

We rode Bus 59 to school and it was constantly breaking down, usually timed with sub-zero mornings. Diane even wrote a guitar song about it stalling out, as the yellow bus was known to die. When it wasn't broken, we had a game we would play with the unwilling bus driver, Lloyd. He had a bald spot on the back of his head. The game rules were: if you hit the driver's seat with a spitball, you made ten points. If you hit him on the shoulders, you got 20 points. If you hit that bald spot, it was a full 30 points. If he caught you and made you sit in the seat behind him, you were the King of the game! Sitting in that seat was a badge of honor for us. Norm won the top honor, though. Who would think "bookworm Norm" would take top honors?

Once when we first started playing this game, Norm was ignoring us. He put a book over his face and was pretending to be asleep. Suddenly, a spit ball landed on my shoulder and Norm jumped up to grab it. He threw it at the bus driver and got the first 30 points out of any of us! The bus driver marched down the aisle yelling, "Who did it???" Everyone pointed at Norm. The driver grabbed Norm's ear, dragged him to the front, and threw him into that first seat. Everyone wanted to be Norm that day.

Of course, it wasn't all fun and games, especially during haircut time.

There were rumors that The Beatles were on shaky ground because John Lennon kept bringing Yoko Ono to band rehearsals. I fondly remember that I wanted long hair like The Beatles before they broke up, and for some reason thought they would cut their hair if they split. So, I wanted to be "cool" while "cool" was still in style, but my father would have no part of long hair.

Dad would get out his electric shears and try giving me a "Marine haircut", which amounted to a brush cut. I used to cry and pout so much about it he finally met me halfway. The result: a "Dutch Boy" haircut with wayward bangs.

I cringed at my grandmother and great aunts telling me how "cute" I was with that haircut, always pinching my cheek and running their hands through my hair.

"Oh look, that's adorable," my grandmother would say. "You look just like Moe Howard!"

I had no idea who Moe Howard was, but I sure didn't want to look like him.

As a result, I plopped in a chair next to my father and with a hypnotized stare, asked him to polish it off and give me the brush cut after all.

• • •

Dad was a US Marine Veteran, and on Saturday evenings as he slowly got drunk, he would tell war stories. He told me once he was living on "borrowed time". I didn't understand what he meant until I was older. All I knew is that he was a hero and an inspiration in my life. He still is.

He was involved in countless campaigns, including Iwo Jima and Guadalcanal. Although he was "fun loving", he was serious when talking about the war. One story that stuck out to me was about him hiding in a water shaft. I have seen references to it in his declassified military documents, so this was not one of his fibs.

According to Dad, the Japanese were chasing him, and he jumped down a well to hide. He said he was in that well for three days! Every time a bucket was lowered for some water, Dad swears he would pee in it. I don't know if that part is true, but it sounds like something he'd do. Finally, he climbed out of that well, shot one enemy who had a flame thrower, grabbed the flame thrower, and got another one who was shooting at Americans with a mortar gun.

That was the same knee mortar gun that sat in our living room for decades; he said he took it as a WWII souvenir. It looked like a simple iron tube to me, and when Dad tried to show me the fingerprints of the burnt Japanese soldier he said were still there, I pretended to see them. I still don't know if the fingerprints were there or not.

I always sensed Dad was secretly troubled about the war, and I could not see why at the time. In a way, we boys were his psychologists, someone he could talk to. For all I know, he may have been talking to himself and blocked our presence from his mind. No one knew what was going on in his head. All I knew is that I wanted to be a "war hero" like my father. At the time, I saw battle as nothing but fame and glory. When you think of it, my father was a "G.I Joe Martell" toy figure in living color!

Dad was a mentor to me without trying. He once said to me, "Never grow anything on your face that grows wild on your ass!" I never knew what he meant by that, but I once repeated it to my mother. She yelled, "Joe, what are you teaching the kids?!" This is just how my dad was. He was the jokester while my mother was the caretaker of us all.

CHAPTER II

THE MOWING MAN

Powering ahead several years, Dave ran into misfortune...*but I delighted in it!* He was grounded for skipping summer school and couldn't leave the property for two weeks, except for going to classes and back. The only problem was Dave had a job for 2 or 3 days during the week. He would drive my parent's riding lawn mower to people's homes and mow their grass.

As luck would have it, our parents asked me to temporarily take over this community job. I gladly accepted it. I realized this was a *very* important duty, as people didn't want their yard to look like Mr. Parker's down the street, who seemed to cultivate burdocks. I knew I could handle it, so I got Dave's list of customer names. I thought if I did a real good job on the lawns, then perhaps I could permanently dethrone Dave from his job and have it all to myself!

The day before I was to begin the job, I drove the lawn-mower to each person's home. I introduced myself as Dave's brother, explained details about my mower to them, then gave them a small brochure about my lawn-cutting experience and why my service is better than Dave's.

Accepting this job accomplished two things. First, it was going to fulfill my childhood dream of shouting just like a Meter Man, as that bug never grew out of me. Two, I was now proving I'm not little "Hunkey" anymore, but rather, *a man!* I could do hard work like my father did. From now on, I was going to ride up to customer's homes on my lawnmower, yell my title out, and then start my job. From this point on, I was to be called… *The Mowing Man!*

• • •

My career as The Mowing Man started Tuesday morning. At 7:00am, I sat on the edge of my bed, then gazed out the bedroom window. The morning sun shone on my face and lit up my forehead. Dragonflies danced outside my window, foretelling snippets of happiness to come. The weather report for the day called for bright sun with an eventual high of 80 degrees. *Perfect* grass-mowing conditions!

I popped up to my feet, slipped on some knee-knocker shorts, brushed my teeth, and gingerly bopped into the kitchen.

After a bowl of Frosted Flakes and a can of Yoohoo, I went outside and hung a sign on the back of the lawnmower, reading: **"CAWSHUN MOWIN MAN."** I plopped down on the seat.

I looked at a clipboard I left on the hood the night before. I had the names of five customers, two of which cancelled. "That's okay," I said to myself, "just three customers the first day on the job will be a snap." I hung the clipboard on a loose screw protruding from the hood.

The Ordanskis

My first customer was Mr. and Mrs. Ordanski. I started up the mower and puttered down the road to their house.

I never had the pleasure of meeting the Ordanski's. Yesterday when I stopped at their house for introductions, they weren't home. All I knew about the secluded couple was what I heard. They were an elderly couple who emigrated here from Russia or Ukraine thirty years prior. They spoke broken English, but sometimes you could make out what they said if you listened hard enough.

I never knew their age, I guess no one really did. You'd ask Mr. Ordanski his age and he would spit out, "Me, yeighty years old, wife, yeighty too!"

No one knew if he meant "Yeighty *too*" or "Yeighty *two*". But everyone figured that they had to be well into their 90's, seeing how they had been "Yeighty" and "Yeighty *too*" for the past 14 years.

I pulled into their driveway. I turned off the lawnmower and then did what I practiced doing all week in front of the mirror. I yelled out with my squeaky, pre-pubescent voice, "Mowing Man!"

Silence.

Again, "Mowwwwinnnnng Mannnnnnn!" Still nothing. "*Oh well*", I said to myself and started to cut the grass unnoticed, much like how a lone Meter Man would work.

After making one complete sweep of the front yard, I watched as Mr. Ordanski slowly pushed open his limp screen door. Mr. Ordanski was a short, stout balding man with a five o'clock shadow. He wore gray slacks which were cut off just below his knees and carried a flyswatter.

I drove up to him and shut off the motor. "Hello," I said with a smile, "you must be Mr. Ordanski. My name is Steve, Dave's brother. He can't make it today so I'm filling in. Let me tell you about this mower." I slapped the hood. "This beauty has a Briggs and Stratton..."

"BOY!" he suddenly blasted out, "You speak up, me no hear good." He swatted a fly on my shoulder with his swatter.

"Oh!" That startled me. I then repeated loudly, "THIS MOWER HAS A BRIGGS AND STRATTON MOTOR. IT'S KIND OF OLD, BUT IT WORKS," I giggled.

Mr. Ordanski squinted his eyes, seemingly confused. "Boy, you follow me. Me, ahhhh, show you where to cut…machine." He used his swatter to chase a moth from his shirt.

"Right," I said, thinking that he was just going to show me where to mow. He did just that. Shuffling in front of me, he showed me the exact path to mow, occasionally bending down to toss a fish carcass out of the way. It usually landed in the path of my next sweep. He made a one-hour job last almost three.

I finally finished and parked the lawnmower in his driveway. Mr. Ordanski fumbled into the house. I was hoping he was going into his home to get me some money, any money.

Suddenly, I heard Mrs. Ordanski yell something in their native tongue. Mr. Ordanski yelled back. I heard a pot hit the wall, and it bounced out the open door. Then silence filled the air.

Mr. Ordanski shuffled out of the house, smiling and fanning flies as if nothing happened.

"Boy," he huffed, "you, inside. Wife sayyyy, you…" He made a motion as if he were eating.

I knew what he meant, but I played dumb: "OH, YOU THINK I SHOULD LEAVE NOW? HAVE A NICE DAY. I'LL MAIL THE BILL."

He tapped my chest with his flyswatter, "Boy, you inside, eat."

I pointed at myself incredulously, "WHAT, ME, EAT? NO-NO, NO THANK YOU."

The old man turned sour, "Yes Boy, you eat." He pulled a crinkled slip of paper out of his baggy shorts and handed it to me. It read: "It is an honor to feed you, and an insult to refuse our offer."

Oh, I see you've done this before, I thought, then handed him back the paper. I nodded. "OKAY, I WILL ACCEPT YOUR GENEROUS OFFER." I tried to force a smile, as I didn't want to insult the man. I climbed off the lawnmower and followed his slow shuffle into the house, mimicking his micro steps.

Mr. Ordanski set his flyswatter on the kitchen counter. Mrs. Ordanski entered the room, waddling from side to side.

Mrs. Ordanski looked like the image I had in my head. She was a portly, shriveled up, aged lady, who modeled a dingy dress and was obviously lacking a bra. The apron she wore had faded fruit printed on it and was worn from years of leaning on the gas stove.

Mr. Ordanski pointed to her, "Wife," then proudly thumbed his chest, "Me."

"HOW DO YOU DO?" I said with a plastic grin.

Mr. Ordanski turned towards his wife, prompting her, "Nikki."

Giving her best stab at English, Mrs. Ordanski recited, "How do you do, Boy?"

He pulled a chair out from under the kitchen table and patted its seat. "You sit," he said, "eat".

I gulped.

Together they set the table for three, working around me as if I was a statue. Occasionally, I could get the whiff of body odor as they stretched their arms in front of me. I tried to plug my nose by squinting my eyes. Finally, they sat down at the table.

Mr. Ordanski said to his wife, "Nikki, shunna dvt?"

She seemed distraught. "Degata, karp gow novee...choba!"

The two of them rose to their feet. "Boy, excuse," said Mr. Ordanski. They walked into the adjacent room and started arguing again, loudly, and viciously.

I heard Mrs. Ordanski, "Sheto tsyvet eto wo karp!!"

I cringed down, trying to dodge the voices flying overhead. "You gonna take that from her?" I said low, amusing myself.

They continued to argue. A plate smashed. "Go get 'em," I quietly said.

Then silence.

They walked back into the kitchen; Mrs. Ordanski disappeared behind me. I forced a big grin.

Suddenly, sneaking up on me from my blind side, Mrs. Ordanski flopped a huge, dizzy-eyed, smoldering fish in front of me. I almost gagged at the gruesome sight.

"Delicacy," said Mr. Ordanski. "Smoked carp. You eat."

I didn't know if he was asking or telling me. "NO THANK YOU," I gasped, "I JUST HAD CARP FOR BREAKFAST."

It didn't seem to matter what I said, as neither one of them could understand me. Either that or they were doing an Emmy Award acting job at ignoring me. They just sat and smiled while I was talking, and my words seemed to bounce off them.

Mrs. Ordanski started carving the creature up and presented me with half of the tail section.

I glanced up at Mr. Ordanski as his wife sliced the beast. Behind his crusty smirk he seemed to be saying, "Oh boy, Boy, I bet you can't wait to sink your teeth into that flipper!"

Mrs. Ordanski finished dicing the creature and shook her head. "Ledisha dalaanta."

Mr. Ordanski translated, "Ahh, wife say, you guest. You try first."

"ME?!" I asked, pointing at my chest. "AH, WELL - IS THERE SUMPTIN' WRONG WITH IT?" I felt like a court peasant, tasting food for the king to see if it's poisonous.

At that point I became the small talk king of the world, as I tried to stall for time by filling the space with words, any words. I was hoping that either the fish would disappear, or they would fall asleep.

"THE SUN SURE IS BRIGHT TODAY, HUH?" I blasted out. They stared at me. "WE HAD, AH, QUITE A BIT OF RAIN THREE DAYS AGO, DIDN'T WE?" Still no reaction from them. "YES SIR, IF WE GET MORE RAIN, I'LL BE OUT OF A JOB." Mr and Mrs. Ordanski blinked at each other, then returned to me. "OF COURSE, WE NEED THE RAIN FOR GRASS TO GROW."

Mr. Ordanski became impatient, "Hey, Boy! Eat, eh?!"

The end finally came; my stalling just stalled out. I looked at my plate, and the dissected specimen was still there. It didn't swim away.

I took my fork and stabbed a limp piece of fish from my plate. I slowly raised the fork to my mouth with a trembling hand, afraid to part my gums. I glanced at the Ordanski's who stared back at me. I looked at the carp remains on the table in front of me, which amounted to the head and part of the backbone. The eyes on the fish seemed to be saying to me: "Don't eat me Boy, please don't eat me!" I would have been more than happy to answer the fish's plea, if it weren't for two sets of narrow eyes shrinking me down.

The time had come; I heard a drum roll. I closed my eyelids and slowly pushed the tarnished fork full of carp between my lips, then loosely clamped down on it. I sat back in my chair and chewed the fish in my mouth, much like an ass grinding weeds.

I was hoping the carp would taste good and I'd run home and demand my mother make carp for dinner. Not so! It was the most disgusting, oily, slimy, musty, salty, gut wrenching, teeth numbing, throat stuffing thing that man could ever think of placing in his mouth.

I quickly swallowed the carp to get the horrible taste away from my mouth. I prayed that it would stay down, not come back up. I gulped down a glass of some warm fluid in front of me, not really caring what it was.

I slammed the glass down. "REALLY GOOD," I said, forcing a smile with my quivering chin. "TASTE JUST LIKE CHICKEN."

"Good," snapped Mrs. Ordanski, as she stood up and walked outside.

I forced down three more bites, then looked at a watch I didn't have on my wrist, "CHECK OUT THE TIME," I said, still looking for an excuse to leave. "I MUST BE GOING NOW. THANKS FOR…" I stood up and nudged the chair back, pointing at the fish "…THAT THING."

Mr. Ordanski grabbed my extended arm. "No, no go!" he said. I slowly sat back down. Mrs. Ordanski walked back into the room; he said something to her. She then pivoted around and walked back out the door.

A few minutes later, Mrs. Ordanski came back with a tarnished tray full of chocolate covered peanuts. She pushed the carp remains to the side and set the tray on the table.

Mr. Ordanski popped one in his mouth and sat back. "You like?"

"YEAH!" I said without hesitation. I thought the peanuts would be a way to get some of the musty taste out of my mouth. Besides, they finally served something I liked. I popped one in my mouth like Mr. Ordanski.

To my surprise it wasn't crunchy like a peanut but rather bitter and chewy. "OH," I said, "ARE THESE CHOCOLATES COVERED RAISINS?" They looked at each other confused; I shared their look of bewilderment and hung my jaw open. "THEY ARE RAISINS...*RIGHT?*"

Through some psychic connection, Mrs. Ordanski seemed to understand what I said. She again walked into the adjacent room and brought back a round can and handed it to me. I tried to read the words on it, but it was in foreign print. I turned around the can to find the English print. I became pale reading it.

"Oh my gosh," I exclaimed to myself, "Gourmet Chocolate Covered Ants!" It was too late—I already ingested the insect. I turned green.

Mr. Ordanski swiped the can from me, "These good for you, Boy," he said, then flexed one of his saggy biceps. "Make you strong, like bull, eh?"

Mrs. Ordanski slapped her husband in the cheek, "Stutu olstealu emustalu?"

They began arguing again, so I used the fighting as a diversion to scoot out the door. Quickly, I jumped on the lawnmower seat and turned the key.

On the hood of my lawnmower sat two carp with dragon-flies exploring them. Apparently, Mrs. Ordanski found the time to sneak outside and put a couple of "gifts" on my mower for me to take home. I sped down the road and held them down on the hood with my arm, finally stopping the lawnmower and tossing the carp in the ditch. I wiped my slimy hands on my shirt.

Fertilizer for the road weeds, I thought, then sat back down on the lawnmower.

With a sigh, I took my clipboard off from the lawnmower and read the next name. "Mrs. Ross", I muttered to myself. I hung the clipboard back on the screw, slipped the tractor into third gear, and proceeded to her house.

Mrs. Ross

Mrs. Ross was a seventy-four-year-old widowed lady who lived alone in a microhouse. She never left her dwelling very often but would occasionally go to the Big M with a massive number of grocery coupons or perhaps visit the Brewerton Drug store.

The entire town would have recurring nightmares about falling in the checkout line behind her. If this was in your fate, then you might as well pitch a tent and spend the night; she had to do the math for the checkout person, to prove the sardines were five cents off when buying three, or something nit-picky. Everything she owned had to be perfect, never a scratch or mar in her life. Devastation to her was finding a dust-bunny under her sofa.

I pulled my lawnmower into Mrs. Ross's cobblestone driveway. "Mowing Mannn!" I yelled over the puttering mower.

Inside of her house, I saw Mrs. Ross pull back a little corner of her living room curtain. She then disappeared.

I frowned. "Mowing Mannn!" I yelled again. Mrs. Ross opened the door and stepped out on her landing, shaking her fist.

"SHUT THE HELL UP, I HEAR YOU!" she yelled. "AND TURN THAT DAMN THING OFF!!" I turned off the lawnmower.

I said loudly, "I'M HERE, MRS. ROSS, TO MOW YOUR LAWN!"

"Why are you yelling? I'm right here."

I quieted down. "Oh sorry, the last people I mowed grass for couldn't hear good, and I thought maybe—-"

"It's about time you got here!" she snapped. "You're so late, you're running into my afternoon soap!"

"I'm sorry ma'am."

"You said you'd be here at 10:30. It's almost 1:30 now!"

"Forgive me," I pleaded. "I had to cut the Ordanski's grass, then they made me stay for lunch."

"Lunch? she said incredulously, retracting her head. "All they eat are carp and ants, and who's crazy enough to eat that garbage? You even smell like their house."

I sighed.

"In the future - if you even have one with me now - make it a point to get here when you promise."

"Yes ma'am."

"Your brother Dave always makes it here on time. That sweet young man!"

Good 'ol Dave, I thought.

"Now get your feet moving over here and let me show you what to do, Stevie."

"You don't have to call me 'Stevie'. Steve will do just fine."

"Well then quit your yapping and get over here," barked Mrs. Ross. I quickly jumped to attention and joined her.

She showed me where to cut. It was easy: not a big yard, no trees or bushes to maneuver around, and the grass was rather short. *Simple,* I thought. I wanted to spend the least amount of time as possible at her house.

I got on my lawnmower, started it up, and began to mow her yard.

After making one complete sweep of the front yard, I saw Mrs. Ross standing in my mowing lane. She had both her arms folded, tapping one foot and had an angry scowl. I had no choice; I had to stop.

I shut off the motor. "What's wrong Mrs. Ross?" I said as the engine winded down. She ushered me towards her with a pointer finger. "Come here," she said, punctuating her words extra clearly. I gulped.

I followed her to the front of the house. We stopped at a beautiful, undisturbed garden just under the porch windows. "Tell me," She said, "what do you see?"

I suddenly was under her microscope. "What do I see?" I asked.

I panned the garden for five long seconds then said, "I see, ah, roses, and mums, and marigolds."

"Uh huh. What else?" she interjected.

I shrugged my shoulders. "Well, that's all I see. Wait, are those things over there bleeding hearts? My mother loves them!"

Mrs. Ross became impatient. "Look at my wood chips."

"Yep, you got them, too."

"No silly, I mean look at what's on top of them! Grass clippings from *your* grass thrower on *my* wood chips! Now what do you say?"

I was at a loss for words, not knowing what answer she wanted. "Sorry?" I said, half asking and half stating.

"Sorry?" she said. "Just sorry? Sorry isn't good enough for me, young man. Now I busted my behind for hours getting this to look nice. Now you come by and mess it up! Do you know I have a bridge game here at 5:00 this evening?"

I smiled humbly, "Thank you ma'am, but I don't know how to play bridge."

"I'm not asking you over for cards, heaven no! But I want this to look *exactly* the way it did before you came over and ruined it, and *before* the girls get here. Now tell me, what are you going to do about it, huh?"

I sighed.

Fifteen minutes later, I was still on my hands and knees, plucking grass from between chips. The dragonflies teased me as I labored.

Mrs. Ross watched studiously. "You be careful around my marigolds," she instructed. "I think that one's going to spring a white flower. They're worth $10,000 you know! And pull up your shorts, you look like a plumber."

"Yes ma'am," I said, grabbing both sides of my shorts and yanking them towards my chest. I then mumbled, "You old crab."

"What was that?" she questioned.

"Old crab grass," I said aloud, then stood up and wiped the dirt off my hands on my shorts. "I just pulled out some crab grass."

"Uh huh," she said wearily.

"Looks like that's all Mrs. Ross. Sorry if I was any problem to you."

Mrs. Ross cracked a smile and nodded her head, "That's okay, Stevie, as long as you fixed your wrong-doings."

"Just call me Steve," I muttered.

She observed me as I nonchalantly wiped my sweaty forehead with my shirttail. "Are you hot, young man?" Mrs. Ross said sweetly.

"Kind of, yeah," I said. I pointed to the sun and remarked sarcastically, "Just a 'lil heat stroke, but I'll be okay."

"I have just the thing for you," she said glowing. "I made some fresh lemon-aid yesterday. Ice cold."

My mouth watered at the very thought. "That would be great, Mrs. Ross! May I have some?"

Her glow turned into a psychotic scowl, "Don't be a stooge, of course you can! Why the hell do you think I asked you? Come inside."

I followed Mrs. Ross down her polished sidewalk, through her squeak-less door, and into her dust-free foyer. "Your house is very nice," I said.

"Thank you. Put your shoes on the newspaper." I followed her command.

Mrs. Ross walked over to an antique vestibule and snatched a framed picture from it. She handed it to me, "Don't smudge the glass on the frame," she said. "Do you know who this is?"

It was a full size, black and while photograph of a young man in a navy uniform. Stuffed in the corner outside of the glass was another photo of a person in a werewolf costume.

I shook my head, "No ma'am, I have no idea."

She motioned her head to the side, "Come closer to the window, the light's better." I followed her to the living room pane, where rays of sun shined in and lit up the hardwood floor. The window was just outside of two swinging saloon doors. "Now look—-"

I puckered my lips and shook my head, "Sorry ma'am, I still have no idea."

Mrs. Ross grabbed the picture from me. "Well, I suppose you were too young to know him. This man was Mr. Ross, the photo was taken in 1943." A happy-sad smile engulfed her face as she held the photo of Mr. Ross away from herself with extended arms. She gazed deep at it. I witnessed Mrs. Ross' mood suddenly change. I felt a sad aura from her as the air turned tense. Something was about to happen, but I couldn't tell what.

She continued. "He was only 18 when this was taken. Then, two years later, just eight months after the first war, we were married. We wanted a little boy... just like you, Stevie. I guess it just wasn't in God's plans for us, now, was it?" Mrs. Ross let out a light chuckle and then kissed the photo. She held it close to her chest, expelling a long breath. "I loved this man, the only man I ever knew."

"He must have been a great man," I said, matching her quietness, almost as if I were a counselor.

She nodded and looked into space. "Yes, he was. He was. I remember when I met Bob. It was at "The Barkville Halloween Dance". He was a werewolf, and I was a princess."

"Is that the photo in the corner of the frame?" I asked.

She perked up and looked at me, "Why yes Stevie. Do you like it?"

I smiled. "Yeah, it's pretty cool."

She snatched it out of the frame and handed it to me, "Here, take it."

I shook my head, "No Mrs. Ross, no. I couldn't—"

"Go on, take it! I've been looking at it for over ten years. You like it, so it's yours. Besides, it hides the Robert Bryan Ross that I know! Should have got rid of the photo years ago."

I didn't want to argue with her, as I felt as if this was not the moment. I slipped the photo in my back pocket. "Thank you, ma'am."

Mrs. Ross returned to her somber state. "I remember we got our first house together on Oxford Street. We lived there for thirteen years, then it happened…"

Her eyes began to tear up and she looked straight down at her feet. I heard a dead silence.

Mrs. Ross finally said, "The big fire. It burned the entire house…including my Bobby!" She then hid her eyes in her forearm and sniffed.

My heart sank at that moment. Suddenly I felt guilty for all the anger I had bottled up inside of me about Mrs. Ross.

Can this person be that terrible? I thought. I was convinced I was being exposed to a side of Mrs. Ross that no man had ever seen; that I was witnessing a rare spectacle. I was at a total loss of words.

Finally, I squeaked out, "I'm sorry, so, so sorry."

Mrs. Ross sniffed then said, "Nothing we can do about it now". She handed me back the picture then looked up at me. Her happy sad face returned. "After the fire the only thing I could save was that picture. All my memories revolve around it. It's the only thing I have now. I can look at it and make believe I am dancing with Bob again to Glenn Miller or Benny Goodman. Now *that* was music, not this-this crash bang, 'yeah-yeah' garbage you kids listen to now. Can't understand a damn word they say."

A quiescent stillness came over the scene. The only sound was the meticulous ticking of her clock. Mrs. Ross broke the silence. "I'll get your lemonade now Stevie."

She walked through the swinging doors into her kitchen. I was standing only one foot from these doors. Suddenly the doors swung back and knocked my elbow, jarring the picture from my hand. I frantically struggled with the picture, trying to catch a grip on it. Mrs. Ross walked back into the room.

"Stevie, do you want sugar or…*WHAT THE HELL ARE YOU DOING WITH MY PICTURE?!?*" she screamed.

The sudden yelling broke my concentration and the picture crashed on the hardwood floor. I stared in horror at the sight of broken glass and metal strips that were scattered over it. The frame was so old it seemingly exploded. The picture was ripped.

Mrs. Ross's jaw dropped open. "Wha-wha...WHAT DID YOU DO TO MY ROBERT??" She dropped to her knees and leaned over the most intact piece of frame, carefully lifting it up by one corner. I felt lightheaded.

"Oh my gosh! I'm sorry Mrs. Ross!! When the door swung back it hit my..."

"You killed him!!" she blurted out. "What did he ever do to you??"

"Nothing ma'am, I didn't mean to drop it, honest! When you opened the doors, they swung back and then..."

Mrs. Ross snapped her head towards me, her swollen red eyes filled with fiery anger. "Oh, that's right, blame an old lady for your wrongdoings!"

"I said I'm sorry Mrs. Ross! I'll buy you a new one."

"What are you going to do, buy a picture of Bob Ross at a rummage sale?? This was irreplaceable. Priceless! So, what are you going to do now??"

I was lost.

"Well?" she said.

I was searching.

"Well??" she repeated.

I was frantic.

"Well!???" she blasted out.

I was defeated.

Almost an hour later, I was still walking behind a worn push broom in Mrs. Ross's dark basement. With crossed arms she carefully looked on. "That's the entire floor," I said, pushing my broom to one spot and leaving the dusty remains.

"That's very nice young man," she mumbled. "If we had a child, Mr. Ross would have liked our son to do this."

"Right ma'am."

"Although Bob would have showed him how to split the wood better that you did earlier, but I guess you did the best you could."

"Yes ma'am. Look!" I showed her the area between my thumb and pointer finger. "I got blisters on my fingers." I was looking for some type of sympathy. She examined the wound.

"Well good gracious look at that! Just don't pop it here, I don't want blood all over my clean floor."

I frowned. There was a brief silence as I grabbed the broom stick with both hands. Using its vertical position as a resting post, I closed my eyes.

"Don't just stand there, young man, get outside and finish the lawn!"

I clenched my teeth with my eyes still shut, then slowly opened my lids. "Sure thing, ma'am."

Dropping the broom behind me, I dragged my feet up the basement steps with Mrs. Ross only two steps behind. I felt as if I was dragging a ball and chain behind me.

We walked through the garage to the outside of the house where I saw four elderly ladies on the front step ringing the doorbell and knocking on the door. They cradled paper bags and reeked of cheap perfume. I blocked the sun from my eyes to see who they were.

"Why girls," Mrs. Ross said surprised, "is it 5:00 already?"

"Already?" said one of the ladies. She flipped her arm over while still holding her paper bag, squinting her eyes at her watch. "It's almost...5:03!"

Mrs. Ross slapped one of her cheeks in amazement. "Oh, good gracious I must have lost track of time!" She turned toward me. "You can't cut grass now Stevie it's time for bridge. We have to start now before Mrs. Barker's arthritis medication runs out and she slips into rigor mortis."

"Don't worry Mrs. Ross," I said, "I can mow your yard while you're playing cards."

"I know you can Stevie, but I must watch you every second. You get into too much mischief and play with things you shouldn't." My temperature rose to convulsion stage. "Come back tomorrow, okay? But not between 1:30 and 2:00. That's when 'Some Other World' is on.

I tossed my anger filled body on the tractor's seat and started it up. "Yes ma'am, I'll make a note of that." I pulled out of the driveway before I would say something I might regret.

Mrs. Ross joined the other ladies and waved to me, "Goodbye Stevie! I'll see you tomorrow!"

I pulled onto the street, "Whatever," I mumbled, then whipped my head back, "and quit calling me 'Stevie'!"

The day had been a disaster since I looked out my bedroom window that morning. I nearly lost focus of the very idea of why I wanted to be The Mowing Man in the first place: to live out a childhood dream and prove I'm a man. *Should I just turn around and go home*? I thought.

"No," I told myself, "I'm not going to cave in! I am going to be The Mowing Man if it's the last thing I do! And my career is going to start with this very next job."

I continued to chug down the road to my next customer. A smile started to come over me, because I knew this final person is who I waited for all day. My last client would make everything I've been through today well worth it, and I knew that nothing could stop me now.

Miss Shanna

If ever there was an angel on earth, then Miss Shanna had to be it. She was a beautiful single lady, twenty-four years old, who lived in a small trailer house right next to Mrs. Ross. Her income wasn't very much, living off a combination of welfare checks, her ex-husband's child support, and her own under-the-table business: a day care service.

I could talk with Miss Shanna forever! Not only was she pretty, but she was sweet, kind, and caring. She always burnt incense, wore bell bottom jeans, or squeezed into hot pants, and wore a "peace sign" necklace. All her furniture was beanbag and you had to walk through a sheath of plastic pearls to enter the living room.

Someday I wanted to marry a girl just like her, although I never would admit I liked girls in the first place. But my heart pounded at the very thought.

I pulled my lawnmower into Miss Shanna's driveway then stopped at her front door, while dodging a decapitated doll on the grass. I turned the tractor off.

"Mowing Mannnn!" I yelled, then hurdled my body over the mower's side.

I snatched the doll up then leaned down to place it on her front step. I froze in my stooped position, and suddenly I was staring at the smoothest pair of legs I'd ever seen. I followed them up while seductive music raced through my head. At the end of my journey my eyes ended on a smiling Miss Shanna.

"Well hello Mr. Mowing Man, and how are you today?" asked Miss Shanna, glowing from cheek to cheek.

I was without breath but tried to talk. "Ahhh... hi Miss, a, hi! You called me 'Mowing Man', didn't you?" I stood upright.

She chuckled, "Yes I did. Been a busy day today?"

"Yepper, it has been," I hooked my thumbs on both sides of my shorts and smirked, tossing my chest forward. "It's a hard job, being the Mowing Man and all, but I can do it!"

"I'm sure you can, Mr. Martell."

Mr. Martell? I thought, then looked both ways for my father. I suddenly realized she meant me; I was never addressed as "Mr." before.

"You can just call me 'Becky,'" she continued.

My jaw suddenly froze for a second, as I was privileged to call her by her first name. I was now in heaven.

"I know that you know what to do," Miss Shanna said. She pointed towards the front yard, "All of this and the side of the house where the car port is, that should be cut. Don't worry about the tall weeds against the back playpen, I'll deal with that later. Is there anything I could get you before you start?"

"No, Miss Becky," I squinted my eyes, realizing I said her name wrong. "When it comes to grass, I'm number one. I like grass!"

Miss Shanna puckered her lips and smiled, "So do I." I raised an eyebrow. "Okay, when you're done, c'mon in the house. Is $5.00 okay?'

"That's fine…Becky!" I was proud I said her name right. I walked to the lawnmower, started it up, and proceeded to mow her front lawn.

I just finished one complete sweep of the front yard when I noticed Miss Shanna walking briskly towards me, flagging me down with one of her arms.

Won't anyone let me mow further then one circle? I thought, then shut off the mower. "What's wrong, Becky?" I asked.

She sighed then said, "Oh, Mr. Martell, I'm in a terrible position, just terrible!"

"What's wrong?" I asked. "Is there…anything I can do?" I was surprised an offer even left my lips.

"Oh, thank you Mr. Martell, thank you! I knew I could count on you!" I was even more surprised she capitalized on my offer so quickly. I felt like a total, lovesick fool.

Miss Shanna continued. "About three minutes ago, my Aunt Sherry phoned me from a booth in Pennellville. Her car died on her, and Uncle Scott is out on a business trip, so he can't pick her up. She wanted to know if I could pick her up at Greg's Garage, where they're going to tow the car."

I shook my head. "Gee, that's rough. I'd love to help, but I'm too young to drive. My lawnmower is a one-seater. I'm sorry." I thought I had the perfect alibi.

"Ah, but Mr. Martell, you can help!" she exclaimed, then ushered me to follow her around the back of the house. I did.

She took me to a fenced in area, with the only unlocked opening leading to two sliding doors which led into the back of the house. Inside of the fence were five children who ranged in age from three to eight years old. They played with various toys and the baby milled around in a sand box.

Miss Shanna said, "See these children, well, I have to watch them until about 11:00 tonight while their parents are out bowling. I can't very well take them with me, but this is an emergency; I have no other choice than to go. Mr. Martell, do you think you could watch these children for only 1 hour while I rescue Aunt Sherry?" She raised a pointer finger then repeated quietly, "Only 1 hour."

I shook my head. "Geez Becky, I would love to, but I ain't ever watched kids before. I wouldn't know what to do."

Miss Shanna crossed her arms and tilted her head. "Mr. Martell, how old are you?"

"Eleven, going on twelve," I said proudly.

Miss Shanna then reached over to me and squeezed one of my biceps. She said, "Wow! You're really strong for eleven years old…and going on twelve?" She squinted an eye, "You're sure you're not fourteen years old, going on fifteen??" I blushed. "I know that someone as strong and mature as a fourteen-year-old could watch five children. Mr. Martell, please, will you do it?"

I thought for a long second then asked for clarity. "One hour, right?"

She again raised a pointer and mouthed the words, "One."

I looked at her big blue eyes and my heart collapsed. "Oh alright," I nodded.

Her face lit up and she locked both of her hands together. "Oh, thank you Mr. Martell! Thank you!" She kissed me on the cheek. I blushed again.

I followed behind her as she walked through her house and talked at the same time. "Okay, Mr. Martell, here are the rules. The children will play with each other and basically take care of themselves. Don't let them run in and out of the house because I have the air conditioner on." She put her wallet in her purse and continued talking. "The littlest one is baby Bobby. I just changed his diapers. By the time he decides to mess again I'll be back."

Miss Shanna slung her purse around her shoulder and grabbed her car keys. I followed her as she walked to the car. She continued, "If they're hungry I have some granola bars on top of the spice rack, but don't give one to KJ, she's allergic to them. You can give her the candy bar from the white cupboard instead. You got all that Mr. Martell?" She sat down inside her car and put her keys in the ignition.

My head was swarming. "Yeah, right, clear as a bell. But which one is KJ?"

"She's one of the twin girls, with—" she paused and said, "Oh, just ask them, they'll tell you. Gotta go now-can't keep Aunt Sherry waiting!"

Miss Shanna started the car and backed out of the driveway. She sped down the road beeping her horn. "Goodbye sweetheart!' she yelled. I waved back.

She called me sweetheart, I happily thought to myself. Suddenly, I heard screaming and yelling coming from the backyard. I ran through the house to the outdoor playpen, where the dragonflies parted their way. When I arrived one boy had another boy pinned on the ground twisting his leg in a way God never intended it to bend.

"Are you going to touch my Batman doll again!?" yelled the boy on top. The boy on bottom yelled, "Stop it hurts!"

I ran to the boys. One of the little girls saw me. "Masher!" she yelled. Baby Bobby saw me and started crying.

"I'm not a masher," I said while I pried the top boy off the bottom one. I held him to my right side as he continued swinging his arms and thrashing his legs. "Now what's the problem here?" I asked.

The boy who was on bottom sniffed and said, "I don't know who you are sir, but you just saved my life."

"Suck hole!" blasted the boy I was holding.

"Quiet!" I yelled. Everyone turned silent; baby Bobby stopped crying. "Good! Now kids, my name is Steve Martell. You may know me as the Mowing Man. Now Miss Shanna…"

"How do we know that's your real name?" one of little girls said with a snotty overtone.

"Because I'm telling you it is."

"What have you done with Miss Shanna?"

I nodded my head, "That's exactly what I'm about to tell you. Becky had to go somewhere and asked me to watch you guys for a bit."

"Who?" asked the girl.

"Oh, I'm sorry. Miss Shanna. Becky is her real name."

"She's gone!" the little girl yelled.

"Shhhh!" I said, using my hands to soften her voice. I glanced over at Mrs. Ross's home, making sure she wasn't listening. "She's going to be back in a short while. In the meantime, we're all going to play nice together, but before we do, I think we should get to know each other's names."

The boy I pulled off the other one said, "I'm Kevin." He gestured his head towards the other boy he was torturing. "That wimp's name is Sally."

"That's it," the boy from the bottom said. He clenched his fists and started toward Kevin. I stood in front of Kevin, guarding him from the other boy. Kevin used me as a shield and would stick his tongue out at his assailant from side to side, dodging punches.

I said, "Now both of you settle down." I pointed to the boy from the bottom. "What's your name?"

It's Donnie," he said harshly.

"Good," I said, trying to act cheerful. "Kevin and Donnie, nice to meet you two young men." I looked at the youngest boy sitting in the sand box and putting sand in his diapers. "You must be baby Bobby." I walked over to where the two twin girls sat next to each other. I bent over and put my hands on my knees. "And who might you be?" I asked one of the little girls.

The little girl sitting next to her spat out, "She ain't gonna tell you 'cause her mommy said never to talk to strange men."

"I see," I said. "Good advice. You should never talk to strange men. Then tell me, who might you be?"

The first little girl I spoke to said, "She ain't gonna tell you because HER mommy said to never talk to strange men." I started to get perturbed.

"I'm not strange; I told you my name."

"If you're not strange then how come you smell like fish?"

"Look, you both have the same mother. If you won't tell me your own name, then why don't you tell me your sister's?" I figured that would confuse them. After a moment of silence, I heard from each girl, "She's Jojo." "She's KJ."

"Good," I said. I stood up, "Now we're getting somewhere." I pointed around the playpen. "Kevin, Donnie, Bobby, Jojo, and KJ. Glad to meet you all! Now," I slapped my hands together, "let's all play a game together."

Donnie started to clap. "Yeah, a game!" Baby Bobby copied him.

Jojo said, "I ain't gonna play no game with you."

I leaned down to Jojo with both hands on my knees. "Don't you want to play a game with everyone else?"

"Not with you. Your breath stinks."

I gritted my teeth.

"I'm hungry," blurted out KJ.

"So am I," added Donnie.

"Me too," said Kevin. "I want a chocolate bar." He gestured toward Donnie. "Sally here will have a dead maggot."

"You're gonna get yours José!" yelled a frantic Donnie, trying to attack Kevin. Baby Bobby started to cry. I tried to pry the two wrestling boys from each other.

"See what you started?" said KJ.

"Yeah, everything was fine until you got here," added Jojo. "What did you say your name was again?"

I finally had the two boys separated again. "I ain't gonna tell you," I answered Jojo mockingly.

"Then I'll draw a picture of you." Jojo stuck her tongue out. With that, she grabbed a green crayon and started drawing, eyeing me up with her thumb. I rolled my eyes then addressed the two boys.

"Okay look. You two guys stop your feuding and apologize to each other before I make you both sit in corners and stare, got it?"

"Boy, you're mean," said KJ. Quiet fell upon the playpen.

Donnie was the first to speak. "Kevin I'm sorry I got mad at you. I ain't gonna try to hit you no more."

"Now that was nice," I said. I turned towards Kevin. "Now Kevin, don't you have something to say to Donnie?"

Kevin was silent. I lightly shook him. He finally said, "I'm sorry I said bad things to you and ain't gonna do it no more."

"Now that's two real men," I remarked. "Now I want you to shake hands."

Donnie smiled and reached out his hand to shake Kevin's. Kevin slowly extended his forward and grasped Donnie's hand. Then, Kevin looked Donnie square in the eyes and said behind a clenched grin, "You dweeb."

"I tried!" cried out Donnie, as he tried to struggle free from me.

"Okay," I yelled, "that's enough! Donnie, sit by that side of the cage. Kevin, you stay at the other side. Don't you guys even think about moving until I tell you, you can. Got it?!"

Donnie started, "But I didn't..."

"Get to your sides, NOW!" I yelled. The boys dragged their feet to their side of the fence.

"Boy, you're mean," remarked Jojo.

"I'm still hungry," KJ said.

"Okay, okay," I replied, tossing up my hands. "I'm getting you guys something to eat right now, just hold your horses, jeez!"

I searched in the kitchen and finally found the granola bars and the lone chocolate bar. A few minutes later I walked back into the playpen and closed the sliding door. I started to hand the bars out to the kids: "This is for you Donnie, here's one for you Bobby, this is for you Kevin, this is for KJ, and last but not least, Jojo. Now put the wrappers in-"

"Hey!" Kevin shouted, "what do you call this?"

"It's a granola bar," I said.

"I don't like these. I hate them!"

"Stop whining and eat it like a man," Donnie added, chomping on his.

"No way," Kevin retaliated. "How come KJ gets a candy bar, and we have to eat this bird feed?"

KJ examined her candy bar.

"Yeah," Jojo added, "What kind of sitter are you anyway?"

I answered, "Look, it has to be that way. KJ can't eat granola bars and we only have one candy bar left."

Jojo shrunk me down with her eyes. "Na uh, I bet there's more and you're gonna share them with your wife."

"Wife? What wife? I never said I was married."

"I'm not going to eat this candy bar," KJ suddenly shot out. Everyone looked at her. "Mommy says that getting candy from boys is the first sign of love. I don't love you. *Yuck!*"

"Don't worry I don't love you either."

"You make me eat this and I'll see you in divorce court!"

I rolled my eyes and shook my head.

Donnie suddenly rang out, singsong, "I smell *pooooopyyyyyy.*"

"Probably your breath," mumbled Kevin.

"WAAAA!!" cried baby Bobby.

"Cat's out of the bag now," KJ remarked.

I walked over to baby Bobby and picked him up, as sand poured out of his diaper onto my leg. The stench from his soiled diapers almost knocked me over. I turned my head.

"Whoo," I said, nearly gagging. I talked to myself, "Becky said this wouldn't happen until she got back. What am I gonna do now?"

"Change him," Jojo said. "I'm not even married, and I know that."

"Anyone know where the diapers are?"

"In the blue bag in the kitchen."

"Can I watch?" Donnie asked.

"No, you can't watch," I said in amazement," this isn't a show."

"Good thinking," Kevin shot in, "he'd probably get in it."

Donnie became infuriated. "That's it, Buster!" he blasted out, then started toward Kevin.

"Get on back!" I screamed at Donnie, still holding baby Bobby to the side. Donnie started to retreat. Bobby started to whine louder.

"Look what you did now," snapped KJ. "You made the little guy cry even more! I'm telling on you!"

"Don't have to," Jojo said. She held up a stick drawing of a person with a big round mouth. "I got him right here."

My head was steaming. I said bluntly, "Look, you kids stay right here until I get back! As for you two guys, no roughhousing, you hear?"

I opened the sliding door and marched into the kitchen with a screaming baby Bobby, every step shaking a puff of sand from his diapers. I found the blue bag Jojo spoke of and grabbed a clean diaper out of it, as baby Bobby still cried his heart out. I laid him on a table and reluctantly unsnapped the pins from the diaper. I turned my head from the sight and smell of the sandy mess then discarded the soiled diaper in the wastebasket.

I never changed diapers before, but I did know that baby powder must be applied to each baby's bottom. Not having access to baby powder, I figured that the flour in the overhead cupboard would substitute just fine. I applied the flour, performed a crude job at pinning the diaper together, and carried a contented baby Bobby back out to the playpen.

In the playpen, I noticed Donnie and Kevin were fighting again, rolling on the ground and rabbit punching each other. I sat baby Bobby back down in the sandbox and jogged over.

"What's going on here?" I asked. "I thought I told you guys to stay away from each other."

KJ took my question. "Donnie is mad 'cause Kevin said he shot Rudolph last year and ate him all up."

"Is that true Kevin?" I asked.

"Yep," Kevin huffed. "Right between the eyes." This comment provoked faster and harder hits from Donnie.

"No, I mean did you say that?" Indirectly he answered my question, so I proceeded to break them up.

After separating the two I looked Donnie square in his bloodshot eyes and talked calmly to him.

"Donnie, Kevin didn't shoot Rudolph..."

"Did so," Kevin blurted out. Donnie and I both ignored him.

I continued, "We all know there's no Santa Claus, so how could Kevin shoot Rudolph, right?"

"There *too* is a Santa Claus!" cried Donnie.

"Boy, you're mean," said Jojo.

While this conversation continued, KJ walked in circles and sniffed the air. "I smell raw cake," she said to herself.

I couldn't believe the "Santa" sentence came out of my mouth, so I quickly tried to correct my words. "I mean, he is real, science has proven that, but Kevin never shot Rudolph."

Jojo remarked snottily, "Why smarty pants, did you get to him first?"

"Look," I said, "Kevin didn't shoot anyone. I didn't shoot anyone. No one shot anyone. I guarantee that Santa Claus is going to come this year, as well as the Easter Bunny and every-one else."

KJ sniffed the air again. "I still smell raw cake."

"Nu uh," said Kevin. He stared Donnie down. "I got Peter Cottontail right in the brain."

"Did not!" yelled Donnie.

Kevin made a pistol out of a pointer and thumb and shot himself in the head, creating a bullet sound. With that action, Donnie's anger heightened considerably. Then Donnie said with a trembling voice, clinching his fist: "Kevin, you no good, son of a...!"

"Don't say it," I warned.

"...lousy mangy..."

"Donnie..."

"*DIPPO!!!*"

Kevin accused wildly, "He said it! He did, he did! He called me the 'D' word!"

"Dippo?" I said, retracting my head. "What's a dippo?"

Jojo couldn't believe her ears. "Oh!" she said, "you're in trouble now!" I'm telling your wife!"

KJ sniffed around baby Bobby. "It's my little brother, HE's the raw cake!" She snapped her head to me. Hatred was in her eyes. "Mommy told me that Hansel and Gretel were just make believe!"

Donnie danced on Kevin's head. "Dippo, you're a Dippo!" Kevin broke free and tackled Donnie.

"Am not!" cried Kevin.

Baby Bobby started crying.

"Stop!" I yelled.

"You're gonna cook my little brother!" KJ yelled.

"I'm not cooking him!" I said while trying to separate the boys from each other.

"What, sauté perhaps?"

The chaos was totally out of control. The playpen became a mad house.

"WAAAAAA!!!!"

"Dippo dippo!"

"Am not!

"Are so!"

"Stop!" I screamed.

"I'm hiding the frying pans."

"Dippo!"

"I said stop!" My sanity hit wits end. All little voices were firing at me from every direction and piercing right through me like fingernails on a chalkboard. I lost all control and yelled at the top of my lungs, "STOP IT RIGHT, *NOWWWWW!!!*"

The playpen turned silent, then:

"Boy, you're mean."

• • •

At ten o'clock that evening inside of Miss Shanna's home, I sat in a living room chair, flipping through a Mad magazine while the window air conditioner hummed. A flapping red ribbon tied to it proved it was running. The children sat on the floor in front of the television paying close attention to a documentary on the life and culture of an African pygmy. Even Donnie and Kevin sat together without touching each other or uttering a sound.

Suddenly a car pulled in the driveway. The headlights reflected on the window, then blinked off. The children traded a glance to one another. Several seconds later, Miss Shanna walked in the door.

"*Hello!*" she sang. "I'm sorry it took so long, Mr. Martell. We had to wait over an hour just for the tow truck. Please forgive me."

Miss Shanna stopped talking and looked at the tranquility of the entire room. Her eyes shifted to the children sitting on the floor, still staring quietly at the television, then she looked at me. I grabbed another magazine from the wicker basket on the side of the chair and started looking at it. Everyone in the room ignored her.

Miss Shanna said, "Is…everything okay here?" The children turned toward her and smiled, then regained their focus on the television. She had an eerie expression on her face. "Mr. Martell, how did everything go?"

I perked up. "Oh fine, just fine. They were like little angels." Miss Shanna looked at the television program the children were watching, now with a mercenary showing a pygmy how to wear a collared shirt.

Miss Shanna became overly concerned with the white noise. She said with a trembling voice, "Okay, what's going on here? This is all too weird."

I rose off the chair and tossed the magazine on the seat. I said while yawning and stretching, "Well, it's been a good long day, so I'll be heading home now. Can't mow grass in the dark. Have a good evening, Becky. Goodbye kids."

They turned towards me and said in rough unison, "Goodnight, Mr. Martell."

Miss Shanna didn't know what to make out of the entire scene. I started to walk towards the door.

She stopped me and said, "Wait Mr. Martell, you are going to come back tomorrow to finish my lawn, aren't you?"

I chuckled. "No, Becky, no. Dave should be out on parole soon and finish it. I think you've seen the last of this Mowing Man. Good evening, Becky." I walked out the door and hopped on the tractor, turned it on, flicked on the headlights, and headed home.

Becky looked back to the children. Kevin was the first one to break the silence.

"Is he...gone?" he asked. Miss Shanna nodded her head.

Donnie jumped up and ran to the door, locking it. He then flattened his back and arms against it, *"Don't ever leave us here alone with that guy again!"* he said frantically.

Miss Shanna was in shock. "What did he do? Did he touch you??"

KJ said, "Well, no."

"Did he hurt you?"

Again, KJ said, "Well, no, not at all."

"Then what was the problem?"

Jojo said, "It's not what he did, it's what he *could* have done."

Miss Shanna was totally confused. "You guys are making no sense at all; you know that don't you?"

"C'mon," said Kevin, "you know what happens to him whenever he gets mad. Everybody knows."

Miss Shanna chuckled. "Why, he's just like you or me."

"Yeah?" snapped Jojo, "then take a look at him the last time kids made noise!"

She handed Miss Shanna a photograph of a werewolf.

I pulled the lawnmower in our garage and turned it off. I sat still in the seat for a minute and closed my eyes. Then, after rolling off the seat, I took the sign I had hung on the back of the lawnmower and broke it over my knee. I tossed it in the trash and dragged my feet into the house. It was back to the soup line for me.

CHAPTER III

ROCK, ROLL & GUILT

My high school years were fun, carefree, and exciting, much like my early years but with more independence. I enjoyed socializing, telling jokes, and trying my hardest to be witty. I was quite jovial, a trait I inherited from my father. My friends Norm and Jim Zollo often would do public "comedy routines" with me. Norm and I hosted talent shows, and acted in plays and musicals.

Norm and I never did anything malicious or vandalize property at Paul V. Moore High School, but we did practical jokes, like opening an envelope of flying ants on our music teacher's desk. We made chalk outlines of imaginary dead bodies in the hall, walked down the hallway chanting in a low dirge dressed like monks, and did amusing promos in the morning announcements about our upcoming high school plays or shows.

We had one history teacher that always brought in a metal lunch box shaped like a barn; he doubled as the head of our Varsity Club. We stole it and left him a ransom note in cut-out letters. It read that unless he included a Mr. Microphone for first place in a talent show we were hosting, we would crush it into a sardine can. It worked; we got the Mr. Microphone, and he got his lunchbox back with a peanut butter sandwich in it and an expired coupon for Yoohoo.

I used to be in track and was a pole-vaulter. I would sprint down a runway with a pole and flip over a bar. I was not a distance runner, so that short dash was fine for me. Heck, I don't think I ran over three miles in my entire life. But this was high school and being a "track star" attracted the females, or so I thought.

Once a friend of mine and Norm's, Kevin Schulz, needed a fifth person on his team to be in the Hannibal 24-hour relay. The relay consisted of fifteen coed teams with five members each who would run four laps around the Hannibal High School one-quarter mile track. The runner would then pass a baton to the next person. This would last for a complete day and the winning team would have bragging rights.

One day, Kevin and Norm both approached me in our high school hallway.

"Steve," Kevin said, "we wanna invite you to be on our team for the Hannibal 24-hour Relay. It's a lot of fun! And we need someone with your strength, wisdom, and fortitude!" Kevin smirked at Norm.

"No way," I quickly said, closing my locker and clicking the combination lock. "I heard about that thing. I wouldn't be caught dead doing that…and your corny 'suck-up' words ain't gonna work." I shook my head, "'Wisdom', my ass!"

"But Steve," Norm shot in, "Shannon Pauldine will be there. Last year, it was hot, and they sprayed all the people with a hose when they ran by, including Shannon! Wow, you should have seen that sight!"

Shannon Pauldine was a girl Norm and I went to grade school with, who I had a mad crush on. The joke back then was we were in fourth grade, but she was built like she was in fifth.

I thought for a second then questioned, "Shannon Pauldine?" Norm and Kevin nodded their heads. "A wet t-shirt?" I asked. They grinned and nodded again.

I put two thumbs up, "Sign me up baby, I'm there!"

At the 24-hour relay, the rest of my team was made up of distance runners, who were jogging easily around the track and when they were not jogging, they occasionally ate baby food and slurped honey. If they drank water, they would take a few sips and rinse out their mouth. Me? I would sprint as fast as I could around the track, eat hamburgers, fries and hotdogs from the concession stand and guzzle down Pepsi and Yoohoo.

"Steve," Kevin said, with his jaw hanging open, "what are you doing? You're going to burn yourself out…and your gut's going to explode!"

"Look," I said while wiping mustard off my mouth, "you *pansies* just keep on eating your baby food and waltz around the track. I'm going for the gold, you hear?"

As a result of my cavalier attitude, I passed out in seventeen hours after ralphing my stomach. Oh, and Shannon Pauldine was not even there.

• • •

Shortly after running the relay, my father was diagnosed with stage four lung cancer and given six to eight months to live. He refused to die in the hospital and elected to stay at home. No one knows how he got the cancer, but in the military, he became addicted to cigarettes, which they gave out like candy in WWII.

One of the last things he said to me was, "Hunkey, I don't want any of you boys to join the military, but if you must, never, EVER join the Marines. They're the first ones on the beach and often never get off it. And if they do survive, they may not have all the parts they came with."

My father paused and tried to take a deep breath. He said with a raspy voice, "All your life I taught you how to live; now I'm going to teach you how to die."

One starry evening on October 10, 1979, I joined my siblings around my father and mother, as Dad laid face-up on our sofa. Then, at the young age of 56 years old, my father took his final breaths and gave up the ghost. His last words were, "Have faith."

The man who was a solid feature in my life, the one who taught me right from wrong, was gone. He was an awesome father and a hard-core Marine to the very end.

A month after my father passed away, I made a decision: *I intended to join the Marines after graduation from high school.* I wanted to be like my father. I didn't tell anyone for fear of ridicule from family and friends, especially family.

Now at the age of seventeen, I knew the realities of war and it wasn't my adolescent picture of fame and glory. In high school I learned about veterans having flashbacks about combat action, which fit Dad perfectly. But it was peace time, so I saw combat as a non-issue, with American hostages in Iran being the only national conflict at the time. I wanted to give something back to my country, much like my father did. Besides, if I wanted to go to college, I could for free.

Meanwhile, Norm introduced me to his cousins Eric and Elliott Mattice. All three of them were sick of disco. You would *never* see them wear a silk shirt or have featherback hair, which was traditional disco garb at the time.

"I can't stand that hideous thumping," Elliott used to say. They were inspired by the "anti-disco" local band the Flash Cubes, who go back to basic rock music and power pop with a twist of "state-of-the-art" 1978 technology: hence, New Wave.

The New Wave movement inspired the Mattices to create a band. The only problem was they didn't know how to play instruments. Norm could play a few cords and keep a beat on his father's drum set; Eric could thump a few bass strings and Elliott could finger some guitar lines, but besides that they had no musical talent.

Norm started to learn how to play guitar quickly, as his girlfriend's father was a music teacher and Norm's father played some folk music. So, he would play rhythm guitar, but they still needed a drummer.

My brother Rick taught me how to pound out the theme from "Hawaii Five-O" on drums. I was left-handed and partially ambidextrous, so drumming came easy. These factors caused Norm to ask me to drum. Besides, Ringo Starr was a left-handed drummer, so the guys thought I would make the band seem cooler.

Those guys wanted to be as big as The Rolling Stones; I just saw it as a good crutch to meet girls, the one I had craved since the 60's. Dave gave me a cheap Kingston Drum set with a few cracked Zildjian cymbals. The Mattices decided to name our group "Dress Code" and Elliott painted the logo on my bass drum. We were now ready for "on-the-job-training" as a new wave, punk rock, anti-disco, power-pop type, hybrid band.

Our band had to be clever when practicing; no one wanted to hear us clanging cymbals or trying to synchronize distant cords. As a result, we could not rehearse when anyone's parents were around.

One hot summer day, after being batted around from house to house, we decided to run extension cords from the Mattice's garage and rehearsed in a field next to it. Eric and Elliott's sisters thought it would be a novel idea to put a Juicy-Juice stand up in front of our "rehearsal pasture", thinking we would lure in customers. Seeing how the "customers" were mostly cows and chickens, the sisters sat at their stand and drank most of the beverage themselves.

The field session was a disaster! For some reason, I kept on morphing into a bouncy, "jungle" beat on the drums, as Elliott would say after abruptly stopping his guitar, "Steve, no 'Bo Diddley'!" Eric would try a classic bass guitar line and snarl air through his nose. Norm would be in his own world while trying to figure out licks to the latest Cheap Trick song.

After months of rehearsing in odd places, far away from pedestrian's earshot, we started to sound good, or at least thought we did. Dress Code even started to perform at small venues! Once we played in the deep end of a drained-out, inground swimming pool. We could not be choosy, so we would play *anytime* and *anywhere* we were invited, even if it were in a cement hole.

Shortly after our infamous swimming pool gig, we finally got our first paying job: playing at a Millard Hawk Jr. High dance for $75.00. The three Mattice members split the cash three ways and paid me for gas to transport our equipment. I grudgingly took it. Dan Carroll, a big, strong friend of ours, volunteered to be our "sound man". His job was to turn the volume up and down on our Peavey amps and try to prevent feedback from our screeching noise.

The band job went fairly well, with one small miscue. When we started playing, it was light outside, but after our intermission, the sun went down. Unfortunately, we were in the dark side of the dimly lit room. No one thought about lighting.

The day after the dance, Dan, Norm, and I got together to analyze our inaugural paid gig.

"Hey Dan," I said, "why didn't you turn the lights on so people could see us? I could hardly see my snare drum!"

Dan snarled back to me, "Say, I volunteered to run sound, not flick a light switch. Besides, I couldn't even find the switch! All I can say is if you guys can't afford lightning, then bring flashlights next time." He held his right fist under his head, "Shine it under your chin like this, you'll look like one of the guys from the band 'Queen.'"

Norm shot in, "Right, try doing the flashlight thing while drumming." He turned to me, "And Steve, why did you stop drumming during the middle of 'Do you Want to Dance?'"

I shrugged my shoulders, "I don't know, I thought it was the end of the song."

"End of the song!" Norm exclaimed. "That was just a pause, one we practiced the other day. Remember? You weren't supposed to stop 'cold turkey.'"

I shook my head, "I never got the memo. You three practice things together then tell me to fill in the blanks with beats and clangs and make believe I'm the second coming of Keith Moon."

"Steve, bull crap!" Dan remarked with a stern grin, "First of all, you're no Keith Moon. Second, I was at that same meeting, and yes, you were there. You were too busy checking out a Playboy magazine, so it went right over your head."

"It was YOUR magazine!" I quipped back. Then I smiled, "Speaking of which, did you see that hot chick with her arms crossed during 'Do you Want to Dance'? She was staring at me!"

Norm nudged Dan on the side, "Now we know why he stopped drumming," Dan smiled.

I snapped my head around and looked at both, "No, really, I think she has the hots for me!"

Norm said, "Oh, I bet you mean Mari Grace Ludlow. Forget it Steve, she's got a boyfriend who's a body builder and her mother is a hall monitor. She keeps a close eye on her. Mari is out of your league."

"No way!" I said with a spark. "Then where was her bumble head boyfriend? Not with her, I'll tell you that much."

"Maybe you never got the memo," Dan quipped. Norm grinned. "He was probably at home chewing on some iron. Steve, you take aim at her and he's gonna turn your brain into guacamole. I bench press 300 pounds and even I would think twice about dancing with him."

I frowned and shook my head, "Guys, you just don't know the power of love."

"Maybe not," said Norm, "but we do know about the power of his fist in your right eye socket."

I didn't go out with Mari, though. Instead, I started to go out with this girl named Hazel Pace, a junior at my high school. We meshed together perfectly! We both had things in common, mostly entertainment, and whenever we were together life seemed enchanting. We knew each other's schedule at high school and would "magically" find each other alone in the dark room of photography class. Kissing Hazel under a dark light seemed so perfect, so mystic.

One warm evening we were at the same party at a house on Oneida River. Hazel and I found ourselves hiding and kissing on the dark side of their docked houseboat, while Dan playfully tossed unsuspecting partygoers into the shallow river. The houseboat was the perfect hide-a-way to not become one of Dan's victims.

Our passion for each other grew and grew. Although we were both just dating, we knew our relationship would bloom into something bigger. How big remained to be seen.

While Hazel and I were courting, I was still doing stand-up comedy at different local engagements with Norm, acting and singing. I did barely good enough to pass high school, but basically the world was my playground and Paul V. Moore High School was my stage.

I had no care in the world and always wanted to have the focus on me. My attitude was somewhat cocky, sarcastic at times, but always socializing with kind intent. For whatever reason, I was not happy unless the community or public were happy with me. So, pleasing people gave me a secondary gain of bolstering my ego.

But even eight months later, the death of my father was puzzling to me. I felt guilty having fun with life knowing my father had just died. *I should be mourning more,* I thought. But still, I could not escape the feeling I had watching him die at our house. I was going to graduate from high school in two weeks and knew that I was planning to join the Marines, but I still felt lost with no direction. My life was a mishmash of pleasantries and guilt.

Deep inside, I felt as if my father died with secrets of the war. The "entertainment" angle of his war stories faded from me. When he got drunk and morphed into them, I felt as if his memory was talking out loud. But now joining the Marines became an obsession to me; subconsciously I wanted to see and feel what he went through.

I wish I got to know this man better, I thought to myself.

The night of June fifth, I had a dream about my father. It was brief, but the words from him were solid. He stood in one place, looked at me and said, "Hunkey, you're going to be okay. Things are going to be rough at first, but you're going to be okay. You're going to be something someday." It was that quick, almost like a flashcard. But it seemed so real, just like I was still sitting at the kitchen table, hearing him tell war stories.

I didn't really think too much about this dream, as I had a lot on my mind. Still, I told my sister Patt about it, but just her. I figured she wouldn't think I'm crazy.

When I think back, today, I know more about Post Traumatic Stress Disorder, better known as PTSD. That is what Dad had. Reminiscing about WWII was tattooed on his brain and became a disease. I now understand there is nothing glorious about battle. But my dad was, and remains, my hero and I appreciated his good sense of humor. What I also appreciated, however, is his resilience. It's that resilience and insistence on living a good life that brought him back after the horrors he must have witnessed. It was his sense of humor and general positive attitude that helped him raise eight kids. These are the good traits he passed down to me. To this day, I also use his sense of humor, despite being surrounded by trials and tribulations. Hey, what is life without finding joy in the rubble? And let's face it: there's a lot of rubble to go around.

CHAPTER IV

THE FALL INTO PANDEMONIUM

June 21st, 1980 was my graduation day from high school, but the day before the event we had a commencement rehearsal. Our school advisors showed us how to march to the gymnasium, where to sit and how to angle our caps. The atmosphere was jubilant, as twelve years of education worked up to this moment. Graduation day would be the tipping point from being adolescents to young adults. People passed along yearbooks to scribble one last funny statement or take a stab at philosophical words.

After the rehearsal I drove home in a Chevy Blazer I inherited from my father. I noticed my gas tank was almost empty, and I was broke. I tried to figure out how my fumes would get me to graduation the next morning, let alone back home.

At the same time, my brother Don was doing a sound check before a band job. He phoned me at my mother's house as I watched the news, waiting for the weather, hoping the soggy day would clear up before tomorrow.

"Yo Steve," Don said, as amplifier feedback screeched in the background, "I just got a new puppy; I forgot to put her inside before I left. Could you head over to my place and let her into my trailer house? It's raining out."

I glanced outside through the wet window. "Sure. It's in Caughdenoy, right? How do I get there?"

He told me how to get there and where to find the hidden housekey. Since I was planning on going to a music store anyway to get Norm guitar strings for a graduation present, I didn't mind doing the favor.

I had to beg my mother to use her car because the SUV wasn't going anywhere without gas. My last bit of money was going for the strings. She agreed to let me use it and gave me a ten spot for my own gas, with the promise that I would pick up four cans of tomato sauce on my way back. Naturally, I agreed to these terms, so she gave me an extra ten. I tossed on my simulated leather jacket, zipped it up, then jumped in my mother's car.

I followed Don's directions into the trailer park; it was a tangle of crushed stone roads and occasional mud puddles.

Finally finding his trailer, I located the key beneath the rock he described, let his puppy in the house, locked the front door, then left. I climbed into the car and clicked the seatbelt.

I started the car up, slipped it into drive, then moved forward, splashing through some puddles. I got lost in the maze of dirt roads, so I asked someone in a yellow rain suit holding an umbrella how to get out of the park. She pointed the direction out. Before pulling out, I adjusted the radio to the latest Cheap Trick song, then proceeded down Caughdenoy Road to the music store.

As I drove down to road, singing a duet to the song *I Want You to Want Me*, a jarring jolt suddenly rocked my cars' side. I recall my body flinging to the right door of the vehicle. Suddenly, everything went black.

-Then there was nothing-

Eventually, a slow haze cleared in my head, and next thing I remember was being in the television show *Get Smart*. In the intro to that show, there are doors Maxwell Smart walks through that open automatically. I believed I was flying through those doors, feet first.

The reality was that I was seeing the lights on the ceiling of a hospital as I lay on a gurney, being rushed through the emergency room. *My* reality was that I had been in a terrible car crash. As I think back about the accident, I had no idea any of this had happened for at least a month. I would spend the rest of my life recalling things that happened not only that day, but over the next year. As I'm writing this book, I am still recalling things that happened back then.

I was hit broadside by a van. I was only a mile away from Don's house. However, I had the good sense to wear my seatbelt, although no seatbelt law was in effect in New York State at the time. I was still a kid on the adrenaline rush of graduation, so did I run a stop sign? Did I stop and see my way clear, only to misjudge? I may never know. But I do know that the car that hit me slammed into my passenger's door and twisted my mom's car like a pretzel.

My seatbelt broke. The fabric simply gave out. I was tossed around the car like a pinball. My body was thrown to the passenger window. I hit my head, my arms, my legs, my body... nothing was missed. When they found me, my car was flipped over, and I was halfway out of the passenger side window in someone's front yard.

The accident happened on the corner of Route 31 and Caughdenoy Road. My car landed on the roof; the other car had massive front-end damage. Luckily, a resident of the house near that corner called for help and the Clay Fire Department responded. Today, that house stands abandoned. I was lucky that it was not only lived in, but that they were at home.

I don't remember much of the accident, but I do remember rolling. I thought my face was rolling. I remember the *Get Smart* scene, but then nothing after that, because my brain was swelling. I couldn't see. I couldn't hear. I fell into a misty state of conscious, but it was slowly fading. I was in between here and... *somewhere else.* As I lay in the hospital, I heard some super loud noises all around me. They must have been internal because the accident knocked out my hearing, or maybe it was the machines keeping me alive, amplified in my puzzled mind. I'll never know. All I know is that it was a constant screaming inside my head.

As I was being rushed to the hospital, the police called my mother and told her about the car accident. They suggested she get to the Syracuse Medical Hospital emergency room right away. She quizzed them on how I was, but they refused to answer her, and just requested she go immediately to the ER. She dropped the phone then grabbed Jeanmarie, who was at the house when the call came. The woman who had just lost her husband rushed to the hospital to try and hold onto her baby.

But before my mother left, my sister Patt got the panicked call from her. Mom knew I might not live, just because of the silence of the police. Patt's husband Larry rushed Mom and Jeanmarie to the hospital so Patt could stay with the kids. She called Father Joseph Kent in hysterics so he could start a prayer chain.

They scurried into the hospital, only to be restrained from seeing me. Instead, they were briefed on my condition. An ER doctor said when I arrived, I was moaning and thrashing my arms and legs. He also said he didn't know the severity of my injuries, but I seemed to have severe brain trauma. They hadn't yet ruled out internal injuries, so the next few hours would be crucial for me.

My distraught family peeked through a crack in the curtain as I fought the hospital staff, who were trying to insert an intubation tube in me. One of the respiratory therapists knew Jeanmarie and quickly closed the curtain when he noticed her. Another therapist ushered everyone into the waiting room, promising to update them when possible.

Larry called Patt from the waiting room payphone as my mother wept behind him. He emphasized loudly, so my mother would overhear, "I think he's gonna make it, I really do. I just have a feeling."

Norm showed up with his parents around 1:00am and convinced the orderlies he was my brother; my family played along with it. An emergency room resident included him when they told my family their preliminary findings: my head injury was extensive, and I had lapsed into a coma.

My mother dropped her jaw; all eyes were focused on the orderly. He paused, then continued. "We would have to do a partial frontal lobotomy to try to save Steve's life."

The neurosurgeon on call explained that the lobotomy, or lobectomy, was necessary because the main blow to my brain came from the back of my skull. When that back part swells, the pressure to my frontal lobe could permanently damage the base of my brain, causing my heart to stop beating and my breathing to halt. Taking out part of the front of my brain could give it some "wiggle room" to alleviate the pressure. My family was also told that if I live past the first 48 hours I might survive, but I might also be on permanent life support. Even if I did survive and wasn't on life support, the quality of my life was uncertain. But the risk from the partial lobotomy outweighed the other fate.

In mid-morning on June 21ˢᵗ, my classmates joined in their caps and gowns at the high school. News of my car accident swirled everywhere. Several of my closest classmates gathered around Norm, trying to make sense of it all. He told them the grave details, having no idea if I was alive at that moment.

Graduation went on without me. My classmates walked in a straight line into the auditorium with the song *Pomp and Circumstance* blaring in the air. They took their assigned seats. But mine was left empty with a pair of drumsticks and a rose on it.

• • •

As it turned out, my skull was fractured in three areas. My hearing was gone. Brain fluid leaked out of my ear, signaling major brain issues. Meningitis concerns ran rampant. Blood leaked from my mouth; the doctors weren't sure if it was from internal injuries. It turned out to be a broken jaw, so my mouth was wired shut.

Miraculously, the swelling in my brain stopped suddenly. I was a centimeter away from the point of no return. If I had passed that centimeter mark, my breathing and heart would have stopped. Since this never happened, however, I was spared being put on life support. My family was left to hope for the best while fearing for the worst.

It just so happened my sister Jeanmarie was a student at Syracuse Medical Hospital and would frequently check on me. My brother Rick worked in the audiology department there and could sneak away too. They joined my mother daily, praying I would wake up. I did not.

One day, Jeanmarie was looking at a scan of my brain with a neurologist friend. She was shocked by the amount of damage to the brain tissue as her friend pointed out the black part indicating severe swelling on the dominant part of my brain. It occurred to her that I was left-handed, and she told that to the doctor. He looked at the film again and glanced back to her.

"That could make a difference in his ability to have a meaningful recovery," he said. As luck has it, I'm the only one in my family who is left-handed. It seems God was looking out for me from the beginning by wiring my brain differently. Eventually, the doctors felt I had a better than 50% chance of survival.

What happened to me was a brain stem (medulla) injury. It is very rare for a patient to injure the brain stem to my degree and still live. It is deep in the back of the brain, and most people die before injury gets that far. Since my body turned when the car flipped and the base of the back of my skull took the major impact, I got lucky. I was also probably lucky that the doctors had enough foresight to give me a lobotomy.

The medulla controls breathing and heart rate, among other things. The doctors were up front with my mother and informed her that not many people survive this type of injury due to brain swelling. Injuring this part of the brain is not reparable. Truly, I was lucky to make it out alive.

I use the word, "lucky", but I don't know if that's strong enough. There were so many things that pointed to me not making it out alive, yet here I am today. There were so many things that pointed to me never walking again, as you'll see later, yet here I am on my feet. I don't know how I got so lucky. All I know is that there must have been a plan for me. Before that plan could unfold, however, I had to experience true hell.

• • •

Living Hell

As my family was worrying over me, trying to look out for me and praying for me, I was in my own separate place. It was like a different dimension away from human life. Although I appeared motionless and in a "comatose" peace, there actually was a freight train going through my mind.

I never knew I was in a coma. I had no idea where I was or why I was in the state I was in. As a matter of fact, I only remembered the *Get Smart* scene well after I was awake. All I know is that I did not feel like a human. I had no arms, no legs, and I just felt like a giant ball of excruciating, intense agony I could not escape. My head area felt as big as a beach ball. I tried to open what I thought were my eyes, but I had no eyes to open. I tried to open my mouth, but I had no mouth to open. I was deaf to the outside world, yet I could hear myself, which remains to this day a strange state of existence.

I was simply "there". I was inside myself. I didn't know it then, but I was waiting to come back to reality, just as my family waited for me to awaken. It's a special kind of hell to be "there", but not know where "there" is, and to be aware, but not know what "aware" is. I can't even say I was in a prison of my own mind, because at least in prison, you can see where you are. This was much deeper than that.

I don't know of anything more terrifying than to think you are dead and the intense pain and torture you're in you will have for the rest of eternity. Even if you have terminal cancer or full-blown AIDS, you may have thoughts like: *Perhaps if I drink a special concoction of raw eggs, tobacco, and grounded aspirin, it will be the magic cure no one thought of.* I never had even this little smidgen of hope.

Here's a question for you, the reader, to ponder: what's worse, living in this silent hell, or having something to entertain you? Well, let me tell you - the silent hell would have been better than the "entertainment" I was exposed to. Or maybe that entertainment *was* hell. The whole time I was in the coma, I was privy to horrifying images. They were so vivid that I thought I was actually living them. Maybe I was.

One of the images was of me standing with my arms and legs tied together. I was in a small white room the size of a square shower stall. Suddenly, four trap doors, high up on each wall, opened and started to fill the room with sand. I tried to scream for someone to help me, but I couldn't open my jaw. The sand would slowly engulf my body, covering my mouth, nose, and eyes until I suffocated. After I suffocated and died, it would all start over again. Repeatedly, I died that way, and I had no escape. The panic was the same every time; the feeling of being crushed by sand was the same. The burning as my lungs struggled for air was the same. Panicky, useless breaths through my nose only yielded sand that scratched away my sinuses, until nothing was left but darkness…followed by the same room again.

Another image came after that. I was crammed into a giant revolving drum. Think of an industrial dryer. Suddenly, I was surrounded by bits and pieces of other people. The drum would start revolving and the mutilated bodies would start hitting me. Internal organs, body parts, all sizes, and shapes, slammed into me as we churned inside that machine. My arms and legs were still tied together, and I couldn't do anything to get out of the way. I could scream this time, but the sound was muffled inside the drum, and I feared getting a body part in my mouth. I could see the terror on the other faces, in their blood shot eyes. I tried to close my eyes to stop seeing it, but I couldn't. I had no choice but to watch helplessly as these terrified, torn apart souls slammed into me again and again. Intestines slapped my face. I would look away only to see the fear in someone's eyes. There was no where I could look, no where I could escape. I had no choice but to wait for it to end, only for it to start up once again.

I saw my friends and people I cared for lined up on top of a building. One by one, they would jump, and there was nothing I could do to stop them. I would call out their names, but no one would hear me. I couldn't shout because my mouth wouldn't open. I couldn't run to them because my arms and legs were tied together. I was forced to watch as they fell, one by one, splattering on the pavement or bouncing off a parked car. I was forced to see their broken bodies on the concrete below. After the last had jumped, the line would start again.

I'm not alive, I thought to myself. *This is hell. I'm really in hell!!* All during this, there was that same deafening sound like a loud roar or scream that kept fading, then coming back with a screech. Was I hearing my brain? The horror, agony and loneliness were more than I could bear, but I could not awaken from this nightmare. I thought I wanted to die, but I also thought I was already dead. No one could tell me anything. I honestly thought this was my fate for the rest of eternity.

I don't know how I died, I thought, *but this must really be how people feel when they die. How do I get out of it? I'm all alone now. No one to listen to me. What did I do in life that was so bad to put me in this place? God, I'm sorry I stole that Mars Bar from the drug store when I was eight. I'm sorry that I drop-kicked that bullfrog to impress my neighbor friends. Please God, get me out of this hell! Kill me from this death I'm in!*

The hell wasn't just in my visions, either. There was constant agony. I was on pain meds, but I still felt indescribable pulsating pounding in my head. I also felt discomfort of the tracheotomy; it felt like someone was stabbing me. I didn't know what was happening. I remember the irritation of feeling them cleaning that trach tube. I also remember a time when they moved my neck. It was stiff, and the movement hurt. These are the times when I screamed out in pain but could only cry inside my own head. I couldn't scream out loud to let the staff know how much it hurt, and to stop what they were doing to me. I was just a rag doll vulnerable to any probing and cutting.

The visions repeated for I don't know how long. I had no sense of time.

Suddenly, though, I found myself in a soft stillness. It changed like flicking a light switch. It was like I was in a cotton ball. The pain remained with me, but it was quiet. I could see fuzzy railings. They were the hospital bed railings. Suddenly, my father, clear as day, walked alongside the railing. He was shimmering while the room was dull. Someone else was with him. I don't know who the other person was, but I remember he smiled at me.

My father said, "This is my son, Hunkey, good ole Steve. Hunk got into a bad car accident, but he'll get on his feet soon." The whole time Dad talked, the other guy smiled and nodded his head. They also talked to each other under their breath. My father then said, "Okay, Hunkey, we'll try to stop by again."

He reached out to touch me, and I could feel it. The paralyzed part of my body could feel my father's touch. Then they walked away to the opposite side from where they came.

I was shocked. I couldn't believe what I had just seen. Furthermore, I now knew what had happened. But I refused to believe it. *You must be kidding?* I thought. *A car accident?* I figured the vision was just another trick of the Devil, despite the warm feeling it gave me. But it seemed so real.

• • •

The days passed by, and I now had glimpses of consciousness. My body was positioned on the bed so the one ear I could faintly hear with was exposed. I recall fluttering my eyes open just a slit and seeing a friend of mine from high school, Stacy Perry. She was looking at me with glassy eyes, smiling. Because I could sense no body parts and simply felt like a non-human, I was terrified. I thought I had no arms or legs and that she was looking at a corpse.

Another glimpse of consciousness let me see my brother Rick in a chair next to my bed. He spoke to me, clearly stating each word: "Steve, can you hear me? It's your brother Rick. They are going to move you to another room because you're getting better." I then slipped back into my unconscious state.

I was in the bed closest to a line of windows. Although my eyes were closed, I could now sense day and night. I literally counted the time I was in a coma or "hell", by sensing the daylight. However, soon I lost count.

I had no question in my mind that I was in a total abyss. I wanted to sleep to get away from the hell, but when I did the visions were even worse and when I woke up, I was still in hell. I could not escape.

I could feel some needles stab my arm, as areas of my body now had faint feeling. But I couldn't feel my left leg, so I thought that it was either gone, or I was actually dead. I still didn't believe I was alive, even while slowly coming out of the coma. I thought everyone around me was dead and I was still being tortured as they came to see me. Were they saying goodbye to me? Was I in a casket? I was still very confused. The worst part was that no one was offering any explanations, and I couldn't ask any questions. I was alone in nowhere.

During this time, I told myself jokes. I figured that if no one else was going to amuse me, I'd have to do it myself. I also prayed. I apologized for every slight I thought I might have committed against God. I remember Dad saying on his dying bed, "have faith". I asked for help in getting out of this. I asked for answers. I made promises for the future. I just wanted out of hell!

• • •

Roughly a week after Rick spoke to me, I was completely out of my deep coma. I regained consciousness slowly. My right arm was tied to the bed because I could move it somewhat and kept trying to pull the IV's out of my arm. I found my jaw wired shut. A feeding tube ran up my nose and a catheter ran up my nether regions. I was deaf in one ear with fifty percent hearing loss in the other. I was blind in one eye and half my head was smashed in. I was paralyzed on half my body and several pic lines were in both arms. My body was reduced to skin and bones. I constantly trembled like someone with malaria, and spastic contractions were common.

People filled me in on what happened. I was told about the car accident but denied it happened. I shook my head "no". I thought I was still dead and that the Devil was still toying with me. At the same time, though, I was convinced that if I rolled out of my bed and fell out the seventh story window, all the pain would be gone. I tried my best to commit suicide. As a result, the staff tied my right leg to the bed, even though it was paralyzed.

Though I was deeply depressed in the hospital, the shenanigans still didn't end for me. Life always has a few surprises. I remember sometime during my first week in my new hospital room, I was shaken awake around 2:00am by an elderly lady in a hospital gown. She said something to me, but I could not understand her words. The woman pulled the curtains closed surrounding my bed. She suddenly disrobed. This woman, now fully naked, somehow knew how to drop the railing on my bed. At that point she got in my bed and lay next to me, wrapping one leg over mine to try and fit two people on a single person hospital bed. The woman then buried her head in my chest and wrapped her arms around my neck.

I was startled. *What? This is a crazy house!* I thought. *This MUST be hell—nothing like this happens to me in real life!*

With both legs tied down, I was totally vulnerable to anyone. I tried to yell for a nurse, but with my jaw wired shut nothing came from my mouth but a garbled squeak. The woman responded to my distorted shriek by kissing me on the cheek.

I laid to the right of the woman and the nurse call button was on her left side. However, my right arm was no longer tied down, as I promised to not yank out any more tubes. Besides, I learned whatever tube I took out, the nurses would just put another one back in, and it hurt worse going in!

With my new free arm, I swung it around her and fished around for the call button. I then remembered that the cord to the button was tied around the railing and the woman lowered the railing, pulling the call button to the edge of the bed. This caused me to suck in a deep breath and twist my torso over the woman with every inch of strength, still with my legs tied down, resembling a Gumby doll.

Suddenly, I heard footsteps and the curtain flung open. It was a night nurse.

"Evelyn, there you are!" said the nurse. I tried to look up, but my limp head fell onto the woman's right boob. "I see you're feeling better Steve, huh?" The nurse rolled me over on my back and gently ushered the woman off my bed, helping her put her gown back on.

Despite the awkward state I was in, I still felt embarrassed. I tried to utter the words through clenched teeth: *"It's not what you think! This person crawled in my bed, and I tried to page you. Honest!"* However, I still couldn't talk. The words remained a thought.

"Let's go back to bed Evelyn," I heard the nurse say with a smirk, as she put my bed railing back up. "I know this is not you, but the aneurism talking. But it's been a long time since you were with a young stud, huh?" The woman nodded as the nurse ushered her out the door.

Still embarrassed, but smiling inside, I realized that I could turn my upper trunk! It took all my strength to do so, but it was something unheard of just two weeks prior. Unfortunately, ten minutes later, two nurses came back into my room and tied my right arm down again. One nurse shook her head and said while making a half knot, "Steve, all this time we thought we could trust you." My eyes widened and I exclaimed a whining sound. I was a victim of circumstance.

I could slightly feel the right side of my body now and my pain was just secluded to my forehead, as it became duller as the days passed by. I was now getting anxious, wondering how long I would be in this state, if not forever. I wanted to get back behind the drums but still didn't know if my existence was real to begin with.

My busted jaw was still wired shut, so my Aunt Joan cut out the back of a soda box and drew the alphabet on it. I could now point to the letters and spell words if someone cradled my limp arm. I finally had rough communication. However, I still denied everything was real. Finally, Dan Carroll brought in a tape of graduation.

He first played a part where Chris, our class president, delivered a speech, requesting that classmates pray for me, followed by a moment of silence. Then, shortly after, the salutatorian of our class, Norm, announced I would be "okay". The entire gymnasium erupted into applause. Norm later told me for all he knew I was going to die during or after the ceremony, but he knew that I would not want the rest of my class to be upset during graduation.

After hearing the tape, I spelled out for someone to get me a mirror. A person returned with one, held it in front of me, and I gazed at my face. I saw a disfigured person, sucked in cheeks with tubes up my nose, jaw wired shut and an egg for a forehead. I did not recognize this person and thought I would be too grotesque for a freak show.

At the same time, I remembered my father, skinny and frail, about to die. His words came back to me: "Hunkey, all your life I taught you how to live; now I'm going to teach you how to die." I felt as if my father prepared me for this day.

I spelled out for everyone to leave my room. I finally believed what I didn't want to believe: _it was all true!_ I now went from denying reality to acknowledging the surreal truth. I broke down in silent hysterics.

· · ·

The next few days I tried to process what happened. I was confused because the little things I used to do like sit up, stand, or kneel were nothing but a dream now. I was a rag doll of a person. I tried to move the body parts I always could—arms, legs, fingers—they were now dead, slabs of useless meat attached to my body. I could just move my right arm and twist my body, as I learned from my previous bed buddy.

One day I concentrated on trying to get my right foot to move, but it was useless. Then about 6:30 that evening, after my family and friends left, my right toe moved slightly. Although it was covered with a blanket and my leg was tied to the bed railing, I could feel it move and saw a bump under my sheet shift. That was a small victory but gave me little confidence that anything else would move, as it took me all day to even do that.

I kept spelling out on my letter board that if I never walk again, I want someone to kill me, because I'm not a real man. I spelled this out to everyone who came to see me in the hospital: **"K-i-l-l m-e…k-i-l-l m-e".**

Dan Carroll once visited me in the hospital and was sick of my persistent murder request. "Okay Steve, enough!" he said sharply, "I'll kill you later. For now, get better".

Norm, Elliott, and Eric would often come to see me, giving me encouragement to get better and said they would not play out until I could drum again. Elliott, who had the gift of art, made a "get well" card for me and several local musicians and followers signed it.

I felt as if I would not get better. Furthermore, I did not know what "get better" was. I spelled out to Eric, Elliott and Norm, "...a-n-d t-h-e b-a-n-d p-l-a-y-e-d o-n. G-e-t a-n-o-t-h-e-r d-r-u-m-m-e-r." Eric frowned and said, "We'll wait", and Elliott added, "You're our Ringo. There is no other drummer."

My body was not normal, so in my mind if I did "normal" things, then I could ignore my abnormal body, or at least try to. Hazel would frequently come to see me in the hospital. I decided to do something bold, something I wanted to do before my car accident.

I summoned my brother Don to shave my face so I could look my best, as I knew Hazel was coming in later that day. As Don shaved me, he said, "Know what Dad used to say: 'Never grow anything on your face that grows wild on your ass'." My mind said the words in unison as Don recited them.

Hazel finally came to my hospital room. I had her cradle my limp hand and I pointed out the words on the spelling board, **"W-o-u-l-d y-o-u b-e m-y g-i-r-l f-r-i-e-n-d?"** She smiled and nodded her head yes. *I now felt as if someone still could see me as a human who has redeeming value and not a freak.*

Dating back days earlier, when I was still in my coma, my family found out that the initial police report said that I was not wearing my seatbelt. In fact, I was, because even though there was no seatbelt law at the time, I just always wore it. The day after the accident, the seatbelt was found intact in the buckle, however, it was torn from the rest of the belt. Sadly, there was no proof that someone did not come during the night, rip it apart, and then engage it, making it look like I was wearing it when I wasn't.

Unwittingly, the doctors helped with that, reporting about the abrasions. Perfect, indisputable proof that I was wearing my seatbelt surfaced. Bruises on my neck, chest and lap appeared, just like I was still wearing the seatbelt. Immediately after the accident, my brother Rick took pictures of my bruised body before the marks disappeared days later. I had a strong lawsuit.

I was now fully conscious and aware of reality, so my mother filed a lawsuit for me against the automobile manufacturer. But my fractured healing would come well before my lawsuit matured.

CHAPTER V

CHAOS

As the weeks went by, I got more and more movement. I was not strong enough to walk and had zero balance, so I was confined to a wheelchair. Because half my body was paralyzed vertically, I could not move the chair using both hands on the traditional big, rear wheels. I had to improvise by kicking my one good leg on the ground and using my one good arm on the right wheel to propel myself forward. Dr. Jimkee, my Internal Medicine doctor, wanted me to get as much activity as possible, so he did not want me to rely on an electric chair. Also, my jaw healed, so I was freed of the wires closing it. It was great drinking water again, as long as I used a straw so I wouldn't slobber it down my chin.

Dr. Jimkee told me that if I worked hard in physical therapy, I would walk again. I was still in the Syracuse Medical

Hospital as an inpatient but could go home on the weekends if I did not "act out" and returned by 7:30pm that Sunday evening. This was considered a behavioral management version of a "reward system" or token society, and the token was a weekend furlough.

It's important to remember that, even though I was awake and seemed to be healing, I was still trying to work out how I felt about the entire scene. I still carried feelings with me, like weeks before when I was tied to the hospital bed. I felt nothing short of exposed back then. People would come to see me as I was tied spread eagle on this bed. An independent, headstrong young man had been reduced to a sideshow spectacle. I still felt as if I was that freakshow person.

I also carried feelings of being labeled a "moron" and that my life was now over. I had lost all my independence and was now being told what to do, when to do it, and how to do it. I had permissions only if I complied to what I was told. Sure, I was on my way to healing physically, but mentally, I was a mess and all over the map.

I looked forward to going home on the weekends. Not only could I see family and friends, but I could eat my mother's most excellent spaghetti and meat sauce. I must admit, I was distraught when I came home to my mother's delicious pasta, only to see her put it in a blender and turn it into paste. Doctor's orders: he can eat soft food if it's pureed.

One time at home I even caused a little bit of laughter. I was trying to get up the crude, wobbly, plywood ramp to our house by myself, but there was a slight gap that caught my wheel. I tried to pull myself free instead of asking for help, but that wheel held tight. I slid sideways down the ramp before someone came out to catch me. An observer of this chuckled and said, "Steve is back to his old self, always making people laugh!"

But I wondered, *were people laughing with me or at me?* Because I wasn't laughing. It wasn't a joke. Instead, I was trying to show independence with my new body, new image, and new life, but not amuse anyone. But even the simplest thing like moving my chair up a ramp I could not do. It seemed the more independence I tried to show, the more *dependence* was exposed. This embarrassment caused me to become a hermit to the public eye.

But now people were asked not to come and see me at the hospital during the weekdays, as they wanted me to concentrate on my rehabilitation. It made for a lonely week and would have been lonelier if not for my siblings and my girlfriend.

My sister Diane worked part time in the food court at the hospital, so she would give me extra French fries or perhaps sneak me a Hoffman hotdog. I don't think she knew the rule that all solid food had to be pureed, so reading this might be a shock to her. I credit her for fattening up my skeleton; I can't fathom my sister pureeing my hot dog!

My entire hospital week was physical therapy, occupational therapy, speech therapy and French fries. I then would "kick-wheel" my chair to my room and look out my 7th *floor window at dusk, watching the lights of the hotel across the way go on.* Entertainment was predicting which light would go on next. Every night at 7:00 Hazel would call me on one of two pay phones (which ever one she could get through on) and I would patiently wait for a phone to ring. That 7:00 phone call was the highlight of my day. This would be my "normal" weekday for the next five months.

Most of my friends went off to their freshman year of college. Norm, who had a genius I.Q., went to a local college, did not attend classes, and dropped out in three weeks. The band waited for me to get better, getting fill-in drummers like my brother Rick. Grudgingly, they got a full-time drummer. My girlfriend, Hazel, who was now a senior in my high school, was the only one around. I leaned heavily on her. She became more than just a girlfriend; she shouldered my emotional, physical, and at times, mental wellbeing.

One morning in early December 1980, I watched aimlessly as the snow softly fell outside my hospital window. My mood was actually jovial. My brother Mike and my mother were going to pick me up a few days before Christmas Eve, and I would be away from the hospital until that following Monday. I would be with Hazel all Christmas day and perhaps go shopping with her Christmas Eve along with her friend Cindy and boyfriend,

Tim. Tim would be the work horse, pushing me in my wheelchair and my lap would be the shopping cart. Tim and I had it all planned out!

That afternoon, I glanced over my shoulder and saw Dr. Jimkee. He watched me roll around on the raised mat in physical therapy, with ankle weights wrapped around my arms, trying to range my partially paralyzed limbs.

I was done with therapy for the day. My physical therapist helped me transfer from the mat to my wheelchair. With a crooked smile, I kicked wheeled my chair to my room, but Dr. Jimkee blocked me as I traveled down the hall.

"Hello young man", he said to me, "I see you're working hard in therapy."

"Yepper," I said in my best jolly tone. "En-route to walk out of here!"

He smiled. "Steve, I want to talk to you in my office."

"You sound like my grade school principal. Where's your office?"

Dr. Jimkee walked behind me and pushed my wheelchair into an empty room. "Here's my office," he clicked on the light. "This will do for now."

He sat in a chair across from me, leaning forward and dropped his head. "Steve," he said with a sigh, "you've been here for, what, six months?"

I chimed in, "Ah, seven months if you count the coma."

Dr. Jimkee raised his head and smiled, "Okay, seven months then. I've been monitoring you in physical therapy all this time, and you have worked hard, you really have. But…" He paused, looked down again, then gazed back up to me with dark, sympathetic eyebrows, straight across his shady eyes, "But you seemed to have plateaued in the last month, or have not progressed much. So, at this point, I hate to say, I don't know if you will ever walk out of here."

My smile was washed out, "Ahh, what do you mean?" I mumbled.

"Well, this rehab ward is only two hallways long and we don't have a lot of beds. We have a waiting list a mile long for people to get in here, people who have the potential to get better. But if someone reached their maximum and are holding up recovery for other people, they would be a big person to yield the right of way and give up their bed."

I swallowed hard, "Are you saying…*I should do that?*"

Dr. Jimkee nodded his head, "I thought by now you would be walking, I really did. I'm telling you this now because I'm going on vacation starting tomorrow for four weeks, and I know someone who has been waiting a long time and we would like to get him in here in two weeks."

I turned silent and looked down. A tear formed in my eye. I always dreaded hearing these words, afraid they would come, but praying I would never hear them. What would I tell my family? What would I tell my band? What would I tell Hazel? And mostly, what is my future?? At the same time, I thought of all the torment I went through and the empty promises of walking.

The next day about 3:30pm, I sat in my wheelchair looking out my window, pondering my life while waiting for the city lights to come on. Suddenly, a social worker walked in and sat on my bed next to me.

"Steve," he said. "I talked to Dr. Jimkee this morning." He pointed at my wheelchair, "That chair, it's just a generic chair for anyone." The social worker then opened a booklet, smiling, "But these beauties are ones no fault insurance will pay for, customized just for you!"

This is amazing, I thought, *I'm shopping for wheelchairs. I'm not ready for this.* I finally felt total defeat. *That's it, I'm officially a freak.*

I picked out the forest green one, because that was my favorite color.

The word got around that I would never walk again. My family and friends did not agree with what the doctor told me and did nothing but give me encouragement to walk again. However, at the same time, my mother contracted with a construction business to build ramps going into my front door, one in the garage and one inside our house from our dining room to our sunken room. Even the bathroom door was to be widened. This was to be going on during the week when I was in the hospital.

The weekend the construction started, my mother and brother Mike picked me up on Friday to go home for the weekend. My brother Mike told me in a sing-song voice, "We have a *surprise* for you!" When they brought me home, I saw the wooden ramp to the front door completed. "They're going to start the other ramps next week!" My brother said, expecting me to be excited.

My jaw dropped; I had just the opposite reaction then what he thought I'd have. I'm sure my mother could sense my horror at the sight, and she said, "Steven, this is just temporary, to make it easier for us to get you in the house, until you get on your feet." However, this ramp was solid construction; I knew it was no "temporary construction." It signaled a disabled life for me.

When I was growing up, I didn't know many people with disabilities. My brother Mike's handicap was "unseen" to me.

There were a few people with disabilities in our school, but I didn't really pay them any attention. They weren't part of my friend group, and out of my circle. Further, there were people in my school and in my community who were rude and rough on those with obvious disabilities. Back then, we loved to have fun, but there was also the toxic side of my community. We weren't always accepting.

I was aware of this attitude in much of my little, country school district, but ignorant of the emotions a person with a disability might have dealing with this attitude. I guess subconsciously my thoughts were that people with disabilities were content with running under the radar of life. But when I had to choose a wheelchair, and when I saw the construction on our house, something in my brain took me back to all that bullying I had witnessed. Something inside me whispered, "you're a freak now."

Because of society at the time, I had a subconscious fear of becoming a person with a disability, mostly because I saw how I might be treated. I never worried about it before, because, as I said earlier, I thought I would *never* become a person with a disability. But here I was, on the other side of it all. Everything I had been through, and everything I was seeing, pushed that fear to the surface. I was forced to stare it in the face, ***and it scared the hell out of me!***

• • •

My final day of physical therapy in the hospital came, and I would not walk out of there. I lost the game. There would be no fanfare. I was in a room surrounded by physical rehabilitation equipment, as other people lifted weights, ran on treadmills, and ranged their legs.

Why am I even here? I thought, holding a discouraged look. *This place is a joke.*

That day I was assigned to work with a physical therapy intern. She said to me, "Okay Steve, why don't you just sit and see how far you can stretch your left arm. I know you tried to walk, but looking in your chart, I see you reached your full potential weeks ago. So, let's work on our upper strength. You can do these exercises at home in your chair."

Her words hit me like a ton of bricks. Not only had I just ordered a wheelchair, but I was just told the same thing by my doctor: *You're not going to walk.* It was like a conspiracy all medical professionals had against me. They all lied! But for what reason? Just to milk more no-fault insurance money from me? Am I really a "lab rat" to experiment on, to see how much mental torture I can take before I crack?

Like the straw that broke the Egyptian camel's back, her words shattered something inside me. In a fit of anger, I said harshly, "Give me that damn walker!"

It was put in front of me, and I grabbed the handles fiercely. I held on tight and with a sweat, pushed my body up into a standing position, with someone pulling me up by my shorts. I caught my breath for a second, but then, ignoring my wedgie, pushed the walker forward and took two steps. Then, two more steps... then two more. This was followed by another two. The intern then tried to pivot me around to walk back to my chair. I waved her back and demanded, "No!" I did it myself.

I fell back in my chair, dizzy and disoriented from the exertion. I wasn't about to tell anyone I was dizzy, though. Through my foggy mind I heard a muffled, "You did it! Good job Steve! Way to go!" I got a low spatter of applause from the room. I was so proud that I stood up and did it again, this time for the last time. The therapy room was spinning in a mosaic of fog, and I knew I had enough excitement for the day. However, for the first time in so many months, I caught a ray of dignity.

But that was it - with renewed gumption - I was determined to walk, *and no "doomsday predictions" were going to stop me now!*

These little proud moments were short lived, however, especially as I realized life kept going on without me. My band, Dress Code, put out a four-song extended play 45rpm with original songs. Norm played drums for me, and they dubbed it in the vinyl. The record was dedicated to me and titled "Alone in the Crowd", with all three members on the front cover and a fourth sit-in for me with his head turned away from the camera.

They tried to create a "Paul McCartney is dead" controversy, to make the best out of my absence. As wonderful as they were in insisting on waiting for me, my band members had to grapple with reality: I was crippled for life.

I'm now going home a damaged person and my band knows it, I thought. *So, they're going on without me.* This was a big blow, but it came as no surprise.

I signed out of Syracuse Medical Hospital to free up my bed, but I agreed to have an occupational therapist come see me two times a week. Her name was Karen, and she would help me learn how to walk. We would have occasional aqua therapy in Hazel's swimming pool, weather permitting. I started steps with a shuffle, using a walker, then over weeks tailored down to a quad cane. If you've ever seen a person who had a stroke, you know the shuffle. We had to work on walking "one foot in front of the other."

After six months working with Karen, I was able to walk independently with a single cane if the ground was even and I concentrated on each step. But I could only do so by doing at least one hour of self-inflicted, painful physical therapy. Walking was still slow and awkward with a cane and my left drop foot dragging behind, but at least I was on two legs.

That January I qualified for Social Security Disability (SSD) child benefits from my late father. Because my father was the breadwinner and he was deceased, federal laws allowed his child with a disability to collect his vacant allowances. I now had money coming in monthly. However, I was dependent on taxpayers. I did not want to feel as if I was "freeloading," so I insisted on giving my mother $50.00 a month for rent. A small price for room and board, but a lot when you only get $365.00 a month.

Many of my friends went off to college, and I felt left behind with no direction. But some close friends like Dan Carroll went to college only 40 miles away, so he would travel back to visit on the weekends. Dan could sense my confused state. Being a good friend, he would do his best to lift my spirits, like once taking me to the Indianapolis 500. We camped overnight in Dan's truck in the infield called "The Snake Pit."

I remember in The Snake Pit we were surrounded by 1000's of people just hanging out partying, watching the time trials. It was impossible for me to walk between them, wobbling around on the uneven ground with my cane and tripping over beer coolers. Dan saw my struggle, so he did the most logical thing, which was to toss me over his shoulder and carry me like a burlap sack of flower. He navigated around the myriad of people, announcing, "Excuse me, pardon me, incoming, coming through…"

In a panic I cried out to Dan, "Hey, don't drop me! Don't drop me!" Well, my plea not to drop me changed when he had to walk around two bikini clad girls sunbathing, when my words changed to, "Drop me now! Drop me now!"

It was great hanging with Dan, and we did have fun times, but when he was away, reality started to come back with a vengeance. Reality like with my band Dress Code. It broke up and the members went their separate ways. Norm joined the band "1-4-5" and moved to Boston with no intention to return to college. Elliott earned a bachelor's degree from Mohawk Community College and became a self-supporting artist. Eric performed retail duties at a local convenience store.

During the time of the band separating, I found myself depending on Hazel for everything. I had bouts of depression and insecurity and figured I'd wade through life with her. I did not want to go *anywhere* without Hazel. She was my security blanket; the one girl I felt that did not care that I was handi-capped. When she was around me, I felt somewhat normal again.

I remember at her high school graduation party she once told a relative, "Say, come over and meet my guy!" Those words made me feel loved, that someone wanted me, that I belonged to some girl. Hazel didn't want to introduce people to "a freak," she wanted to introduce them to "her guy". She was proud of me! Well, at least, I thought she was.

The love I had for Hazel was intense; I could never get her off my mind. My attraction to her started to become obsession. However, as time went on, I found her snapping at me more and more, even about little things. I also found her doing things without me when she could. My presence seemed to become a burden to her. She sometimes would keep things secret, but word of mouth would get back to me. Jealousy raged in my gut, but I would not let her know; I feared she would leave me if I shared my true feelings. Whenever I learned she was in the presence of other guys with me not around, my suspicion grew high, and I felt as if I was losing my connection with the one person who held me together.

I found myself being silent around Hazel because I never knew when she would snap at me. I felt almost as if she wanted me to snap back at *her* to give her an excuse to break up with me. So, I purposely held my temper back; I was always walking on eggshells around her.

Finally, Hazel found her chance to cut ties with me. She was driving with me through a bank drive-through when she hit the curb. I raised my voice slightly and said, "What are you doing? You weren't even watching where you were going!"

At that point she yelled, "That's it, I'm sick of your shit! We're done!!" She whipped the vehicle around and sped down the road to my house. I apologized to her in tears, saying I lost my head.

Hazel stayed silent. Pulling in my driveway, she got out, came around my side of the car, and opened my door. "Get out!" she said with a harsh snarl. I slid out of vehicle. Then she shot out these words: ***"No one will ever love you like I did because no one could stand you like I did!"***

Hazel then got back into the car and took off down my road, leaving me standing alone in my dirt driveway. I felt totally abandoned and flashbacks of me being alone in hell came back. I collapsed on the dusty driveway and curled up on the ground, calling her name and apologizing in the air, crying for her to come back.

My years of deep depression began

I was totally lost without Hazel. I felt as if the last person on earth who could ever lift me from despair left me in the mud. Suicidal thoughts were front and center again. But this time, they were not guarded in the hospital; no longer was I tied to a bed to prevent me from hurling myself out a window. Now I was out in the public to pick and choose how to end my misery. Pick and choose what to do, when to do it, and how to do it. I never wanted to hurt Hazel, but I thought by killing myself she would finally see what she meant to me. I did not care, and I couldn't see, how my death could affect my family and friends. I saw myself as nothing but a teenage wasteland and a burden to society. I was just a footnote of useless energy who ran his course, which ended at the age of eighteen. Hazel made sure I knew my pathetic place in time. The fun in my life was officially over.

To add injury to insult Hazel became engaged about five months after she left me. Apparently, my suspicions were accurate, and this relationship was developing under my nose. I was even invited to her future husband's bachelor party! Boy, that twisted the dagger in my heart. The funny thing is I went to it. Attending that was totally awkward, but I wanted to show I was a good sport. I hoped going to it would promote healing in my heart, but it only increased the notion that I now was a total nothing in this world.

My mother never knew the extent of my depression, but she knew something was not right with me. My expression was flat 24/7 and I was too dejected to cry. I only moped around like a zombie. At a loss of what to do, she paid for me to take driving lessons. My mother was hoping that diverting my attention from Hazel may help some. Indirectly, it did; I needed something to take my mind off the situation and give me some outlet. When the instructor gave me the "all clear" to drive with special adaptive equipment, she helped me put my SUV back on the road.

My friend Norm would come back from Boston occasionally for a holiday or local band job, and I would drive to the bus station to pick him up. I always looked forward to seeing him and I was a bit proud I learned to steer my SUV with one arm. However, I noticed that he was drinking alcohol quite often. Although I had no proof, I suspected he was using drugs, based on his desire of privacy, physical dishevelment, and eccentric nature. He was different than how I always knew him. When he got drunk, he did not make sense. His wit turned into incoherent babble. There were times when no one could find him. The Boston life seemed to change him, and I hated what I saw.

Though I know better now, I took his behavior personally. My depression forced me to blame myself for everything. *Even my best friend was distancing himself away from me,* I thought. I almost felt as if people believed I had some communicable disease, or they could catch my brain injury by standing too close to me.

Although Norm was seemingly on the decline, I would try to stay course on an incline. But at times I felt as if I had to wrestle with some clinicians who still saw me as a clinical case and not a person with redeeming value.

My neurologist told me that I should not try to push myself farther "than my head would allow." In other words, I could psychologically and physically stress myself out. I should be content with a high school degree. He thought I could work in a sheltered workshop, but given my diagnosis, a career was not even an option. I felt as if all my doctors considered college to be out of the question, not just my neurologist.

I was self-conscious about my disability, but I still had the drive to do something with my life. But I didn't know what. I wanted people to think I was doing something. So, I would drive to Penn Can Mall with a little gas money, sit in the parking lot while hiding my face from passersby, then come home. I was too afraid to get out of the car in the community or allow anyone to look at me. I felt as if my handicapped license plates identified me as a lesser person. When at home, I would call

Time and Temperature to have them talk to me, but they never required me to talk back because I was embarrassed at the sluggish way I spoke. There used to be a phone number you could dial that would provide an automated voice that repeated the time and temperature on a loop. For me, it was a way to feel a little less lonely. I also played a handheld football game until I wore it out. These were all little diversions I created to keep my suicidal thoughts at bay, away from the dagger in my heart inflicted by Hazel.

My brother Dave was a drummer in his own band. Sometimes I would beg and plead to him to let me tag along to gigs, which he usually did. When I watched him play drums, I felt a little comfort. However, the next day I would be back in the same lonely state.

My life was leading nowhere. I just could not shake those words Hazel said to me: *"No one will ever love you like I did because no one could stand you like I did!"* They just echoed endlessly in my damaged brain and capped my sorry life.

• • •

The years went by, and I did nothing but survive day-to-day. I then morphed into a time when I could hardly sleep. Nights would go by without any sleep at all. I tried sleeping pills, which would do nothing but give me "artificial sleep" (no REM sleep) for a few hours, but then a "hang over" all day.

Dr. Dougherty, my family doctor, recommended a person that could "re-teach" me how to relax again. Electrodes were attached to the end of my fingertips to a heat sensor and eventually to a digital readout. The theory: if the numbers went up, it meant more blood was going through my veins, generating heat, meaning I was relaxing.

After about five sessions, with little results, the psychologist sat me down and said, "Steve, after looking through your medical records and after consulting Dr. Dougherty, I see no clinical reason for you to not sleep." She tapped her temple, "There must be something going on in here. Steve, what's going on?"

I broke down in tears and shared that all my friends and family were going on in life and I was nothing but some disabled guy, one who has no future. I was embarrassed to go out in public alone now because one side of my head was smashed in; I wobbled a short distance with a cane; I had a huge hearing aid filling my left ear; my left arm was always bent in an awkward angle; my body was constantly quivering with spastic shaking; my right eye was always red and half closed and I talked so incoherently no one could understand me. *I'm disabled now and just a cornerstone in life!*

I went on to say that Hazel was right: *no one is going to love me anymore.* I had my chance for love years ago and now it was gone. No longer was I the popular, charismatic entertainer, musician, comedian who loved making people happy. I was now a lost misfit of society. **I no longer deserved the luxury of sleep because I do nothing to deserve sleep!** I just stay up late, doze 10 minutes with nightmares of being a person with a disability, then wake up in a panic, realizing my nightmares were real. Then I can't go back to sleep.

"So, Steve," she said, "How are you going to change things?"

I shook my head, "I don't know," I mumbled, gazing down with a straight stare. Then I glanced up to her, "But I do know this: I never want anyone to go through what I'm going through. This is living hell and it ain't fun!"

Me vs. the Monster

Around this time, it was ten years since my car accident and my $3,000,000 lawsuit finally came to trial. I was told this was a "slam-dunk" case and that I would most absolutely win, but it may be negotiated down to $1,000,000. *I could handle a "measly" $1,000,000,* I thought sarcastically. I was finally excited that I may be a misfit, but I will be a *RICH* misfit! I thought my wealth would help people ignore my disabilities. I had dreams of owning a night club and have someone else manage it, while getting big rock stars in there, like Elvis Costello and The Cars.

However, I'd be the "big boss" and would have people look up to me. I figured money would surpass looks.

Although the lawyer my mother hired thought we had a powerful case, we still needed to put the accident together. A mere ten years later, when I was interviewed for a local paper, much of the accident was still fuzzy. Even more damning was that initial police report that said I wasn't wearing my seatbelt. However, luck was on my side, and we were able to throw that out with the doctor's report, which documented the bruises caused from wearing the seatbelt.

The case was bifurcated, meaning it was split up into two sections: first, I had to prove that the automobile manufacture was to blame. If they were found to be at fault, then the case would go to a second stage: to put a monetary figure on how much compensation I would get. If the car company was found not negligent, the case would end, and I would lose.

The defendant contended that if I hadn't been wearing that seatbelt, I would have been killed, so in fact the seat belt did its job. Never mind something was obviously defective because the belt ripped on impact. The accident was replicated downstate to prove the defectiveness of the seatbelt - that type of seatbelt was supposed to withstand up to 6,000 pounds of impact. My accident yielded 3,100 pounds of impact. It truly malfunctioned.

Furthermore, the defendant brought in the seatbelt (cloth) manufacture and the buckle maker to try and spread the blame.

During the course of the trial the seatbelt and buckle manufactures were released, so it was just me against the monster.

The defendant's lawyers opened by telling the jury that not every seatbelt will work every time. The jury had to consider if a plastic strip added to the seatbelt would have prevented the disaster. They determined this wasn't the case. At the same time the car company noted a small metal flange on the car punctured the belt and lessened the effectiveness of it. So, the car manufacturer knew about this flaw, but this key fact seemingly went right over the jury's head.

The jury deliberated only twenty minutes and came back, some in tears, with a verdict: *They felt as if the accident was so severe that no seatbelt would have held*, so the monster _was not liable_. The gavel came down: *I lost the lawsuit!* I envisioned the cunning defendant lawyers toasting and laughing about their unlikely win.

The thing was, we thought we'd won. The defendant's attorney's thought we had won. Word has it they started talking about an out-of-court settlement, while the jury was deliberating. This discussion was abruptly halted when the jury marched back into the courtroom.

I came home with my mother from the courthouse after the stunning loss; my brother Rick drove us home from there as the "not liable" verdict still echoed in my head. *I just can't win on anything!* I thought. *Every time I have a dream, it's shot down.*

Rick was speechless and could only shake his head. He dropped us off and went home.

My mother was calm, not saying anything. About five minutes after my brother Rick left, she was sitting across the kitchen table from me, making small talk. Suddenly, without notice, she broke out in hysterical crying and dropped her face in her hands.

"My baby, my baby!!" she cried, "I'm sorry, I'm so sorry. Why did I drag you through this all these years? I wanted to see you all set in life when I die."

My mother's actions took me by shock. I had never seen her like this. The strong, unnerved person I knew, finally folded under life's pressures.

I choked up. Then I quickly got up, wobbled over to my mother with no cane, and balanced on one knee. I held her hand on her bended leg.

"Mom," I said in a whisper. "It's okay…it's okay. Nothing is your fault. You did the best you could with what we had. I'll be okay. I promise you; I will be okay. *I guarantee it.*" I kissed her hand.

The truth of the matter was, deep inside, I had no idea what it was to be "okay." Did I just give my mother a promise I could not deliver? Was the pledge I made with no substance?

The shock of losing my lawsuit was as new to me as it was to her. It was just 90 minutes since the gavel came crashing down and I had no time to process what just happened. Yet, I was able to make this guarantee. The last person who made a guarantee under improbable circumstances was Joe Namath back in the 1969 Super Bowl. Unfortunately, I was no "Broadway Joe."

My family and friends were highly upset, all agreeing the car maker got away with murder. I too was upset, but also could not shake the image of my mother breaking down in tears, as she fell into a deep depression. Her husband dies in October of 1979 and her baby almost dies just eight months later but is disabled for life. *She told me she wanted nothing from my lawsuit but would like cable television.* That's all she wanted in life now. My mother was also having increased medical issues, including uncontrolled diabetes and kidney problems while recovering from congestive heart failure. This devastating loss was just putting more stress on her.

About two weeks after losing my lawsuit the shock of the loss was finally subsiding, and I had to figure out how to orchestrate life on just SSD. I knew it could be done but had no idea how. With a stare I told Jeanmarie how most of my friends went to college, got married, went on with their life, but I'll always be on SSD and sleep in the same bed I did when I was a kid.

Then Jeanmarie "matter-of-factly" asked me, "Well, why don't you go to school like your friends?"

I never even entertained the thought of going to college, as I had a brain injury and when I get tired, I can't think good. All neurologists and doctors warned me not to press the bar too far and discouraged me from exhausting my mind. I bought into them and saw education for "other people," but not for me.

I thought Jeanmarie was nothing short of crazy, or maybe just humoring me. I mean, I still didn't want to get out of the car at the mall! How was I going to mix in with a bunch of kids? Add to that the fact that I was told I shouldn't try to do more with my brain, I felt my sister was just shooting from the hip with her words. I had a head injury-not just a bad hair day-but a bruised brain! When I get too tired, I can't think. I knew people stayed up all night studying for big tests, and that just wasn't for me...*now, was it?*

But what else was I going to do? I already felt like a burden on the public and social system. Eventually, the following thoughts churned in my mind: *You know, I may as well see how far I can push myself. The worst I can do is be in the same situation I am now. I'm all set with SSD for life. Going to school isn't going to take that away, only working will. I'll never work because I was told I can't.*

My mind cleared of thoughts, but then I started thinking again. A dim light popped on: *I got an idea; I'll show my mother I'm going to school! Perhaps that will lift her spirits. It kills me to see her in this forever stupor. I'll give her a smile if I can.*

CHAPTER VI

THE STRUGGLE
FOR REALITY

Through a spot on my transistor radio, I learned about this non-for-profit agency in downtown Syracuse called Educational Opportunity Center (or EOC). This agency provided free, basic education for low-income residents, refugees and anyone who wanted to learn the "basic, basics" of English smarts.

I made a point to let my mother know I wanted to go to college, but first would take quick "brush-up" classes. I know doing this should have made her happy, thinking I'm not just sitting on my hands, but I was surprised when she said, "Be careful, remember what you were told."

Was my mother joining in with the chorus of clinicians chanting to not "exercise" my mind too much? Or was it an automatic response from her because I was the baby of the family and she still saw me as naïve? In any event, this response *was not* what I expected.

My first class was English Grammar. After taking a placement test, I found I had to start "Level 1: Beginners of the English Language." As it was, I was tossed into a class of refugees from Vietnam. Our job was to create a short, five paragraph, twenty-five-line essay of our favorite thing to do in our spare time and why we like it.

This is a cinch, I thought.

Well, after I finished the assignment and it was graded, I found out the students from Vietnam were getting a golden star and going to level two. But me? I was asked to rewrite it until I perfected it. I felt like a kid again, stuck in level 1 of swimming class while Dave impressed girls on the level six diving board!

Totally embarrassed and with my tail between my legs, I dropped out. I was silent about quitting because I was embarrassed to tell my mother. I also realized that the doctors knew more about me then I did about myself. I imagined the doctors saying, "See, we told you, *don't press your luck!* Be happy you're alive and wade through life."

My mother knew my schedule and thought I was going to EOC, but in reality, I was driving to the Brewerton Pier and watching the ducks. I watched them so long I gave them names.

Then I would check my watch for the end of class and go home, bragging to my mother about how good I did that day. I felt so dirty doing this but, in my mind, I had no other option.

I fessed up to Jeanmarie about what I did, but only after her promise that she would not tell mom. She swore to secrecy not to say a word but told me to give it another try. Her suggestion was that I take a placement test at a local school, Onondaga Community College (OCC) to get a fair evaluation of my abilities. Well, it killed me to take another placement test to find out what I already know I don't know, which is everything, so I dismissed the notion. But I hemmed and hawed and watched ducks about two more months, then finally decided to invest the $25.00 to take the test. Again, I knew my mother was looking over my shoulder, so I had to make it look good.

What happened next could have put me off forever, but again, I was lucky. I took the placement test, and... (with a drum roll) ...*I failed miserably!* (Cymbal crash).

I knew I would flunk it and for some reason figured my sister owed me $25.00.

The proctor at the college who administered the test said one thing did surface from it: I had some creative writing ability. She noted my grammar was atrocious and my other academic abilities were in a state of disorder, but with remedial courses in English and math I may be able to go to school. I couldn't help to wonder if she was sincere with her words or just marketing the college to generate revenue.

Grudgingly I took the advice and enrolled in English 099 and Math 099, non-credit courses. Non-credit courses were not too expensive, so I budgeted my money and paid for them.

I had no idea what I was getting into but was pleased to know the classes were comprised of only a few students each. Basically, I had my own instructor. Also, they went at my pace, so I kept plugging away at the lessons until I passed them. It took a while to master the subjects, but I finally got the instructor's blessing. I was able to enroll into "real" college classes.

One disturbing point I learned from my remedial course experience is I had a tough time just writing things or doing anything with a pen. My dominant left arm was paralyzed to the point that I couldn't use it to write. If it came down to baseball or drumming, I could use either arm. For some reason God reserved my left hand only for writing. So, I had to write with my right hand, which made my calligraphy painfully slow and unrecognizable. My letters resembled Egyptian hieroglyphics. I had a strange feeling this would be a problem in the future.

Despite my concerns with writing, I matriculated into a two-year degree program: Human Services. I figured that was the closest I would get to majoring in an entertainment field, because I was dealing with "humans." But I was ready to drop out from the first day. *I didn't expect to succeed.* I was happy to get this far, so dropping classes now was no big deal to me. I felt like I accomplished enough just passing the non-credit courses.

The sheer number of classes I had to take to get an associate's degree was enough to make me give up. Again, my sister Jeanmarie came through. She suggested I put all the classes I must take on a poster next to my bed. "At first it will be overwhelming," she said, "but you should cross off every class you pass and don't focus on what you haven't taken yet. Rather, look at what you mastered and duplicate it. Don't look back! Work for the future."

That was a great plan! Switching my mindset, I now wanted to pass classes, especially since I had mastered the remedial courses. I got this far, didn't I? I thought, *Maybe I should start caring about academics, and see where I can go with this college thing.* There was still something bothering me, though. Something still gnawed at me and made me hesitant to be in an actual classroom, with actual people. This was totally different than being exposed to a few students at one time, which I experienced with the remedial courses.

I was still apprehensive about being seen in public. That confidence just wasn't there. In my mind I remained a misfit, a freak. Hazel's words stayed with me: *"No one could love you like I did because no one could stand you like I did."* I continued to believe she was right, even as I began attending classes. The words seemingly came from some gremlin sitting on my shoulder, whispering them 24-7 in my hearing aid.

I felt that no one could stand me because I had a disability and was disfigured. I was self-conscious and wondered if I would be accepted. I was sure people would just smile and walk away from me, afraid I would talk to them or ask them for money. How was I going to sit in a college classroom? With great hesitation, I started attending classes, convincing myself I would be snubbed by my classmates.

To my surprise, I found just the opposite. My fellow students seemed to want me to pass my classes and socialized with me! In fact, I remember sitting in a classroom with my head down, afraid to look around at the other students. It was the first week of classes, and I sat in the front row so I could hear the instructor better. I kept thinking, *what am I doing here with all these normal people? I'll never be accepted. I can't even take notes!*

Because I was left-handed and my left arm was partially paralyzed, I could not keep pace writing the instructor's words. I knew this was going to be a problem. I tried to use my right hand, but my letters were unrecognizable. It was hard to tape record the lecture because I had little dexterity to toggle between buttons. To make matters worse, from concentrating on taking notes, I missed what the instructor was saying. It became a vicious circle.

At the end of my second class, everyone started picking up their things and leaving, except one girl. She saw me struggle taking notes.

She approached me and the professor and asked if she could help me with notes. Her idea was to write her notes through carbon paper and give me a copy. "It's easy," she said, "and the campus store sells carbon paper for cheap."

This was the first time I felt even remotely accepted at college. This simple act from a stranger immediately boosted my confidence, and it only got better when the other female students agreed to take turns copying notes for me. They would meet before class and decide who would take my notes and on what shift. I swear, once I saw them bicker about who would have the honor to take them for me.

"You got to take Steve's notes last time," I heard a girl say. "It's my turn this time!" This made me feel like a king, and I loved the fact that girls were fighting over me!

My classmates started inviting me to parties and nights out with them. These night clubs were usually disco themed, and I still detested disco. The girls knew this, so they busted my chops by dragging me on the dance floor, in which I would immediately try to catch my balance. They would then circle around me and clap their hands to Gloria Gainer, while spinning colored disco lights disorientated me. My dance floor wobble made me look like a drunken John Travolta, as I hammed it up and pointed towards the ceiling.

I was still looking for the negative parts of mankind, but it was getting harder to see it: *the positive side was standing out too much!* Things were getting better, and my depression was beginning to lift a bit.

I only took two classes that first semester, because I was warned by my neuropsychologist to not take too many at once. As I mentioned before, he didn't think my brain could handle it. To my complete surprise, I passed both: one with a B-, the other with a B+! I was proud I could even pass a college class, despite just squeaking by, and even earned six credits! I couldn't wait to show my mother my grades. When she saw them, I watched her smile for the first time in a year; a tear of joy ran down her face. She gave me warm a hug.

That first semester motivated me so much I decided to take a full twelve credit hours. I had nothing to do during the day and I was bored, so I had all the time in the world to study. In fact, studying and passing classes became my favorite hobby. I knew doctors warned me about taking on too much, but they did not know about the positive supports I would have. Neither did I! Something inside me started to say, *ok, you did that - now what can you do next?*

Whenever I passed a class, I scratched it off the list of courses on my wall, like my sister suggested. When I noticed that 30% of the list was crossed off, I knew I was onto something big. I was finally feeling an upswing in my life. I had no idea how long it would last. I planned to ride it out and see where it would take me.

But the important thing was the hopeless feeling I had started to get hit by arrows of hope. Mind you, I wasn't sure if these arrows punctured that aura of despair or were lame suction cups that stuck to the outside. In any event, they were shooting arrows, and I felt in charge of how far they would pierce. But I never knew what was coming up next as I started my educational journey. Surely, it was time to put sharper arrows in my quiver.

CHAPTER VII

BUILDING MYSELF: RESOURCES FOR REHABILITATION

During one of my classes, I had to take an internship in a human services agency in the community. I couldn't find any agencies that would take me, except a small, upstart independent living center called Arise, Inc. It sounded like a cult to me at first. But then I found out it was run by two able bodied people and several people with disabilities, all with different handicaps. This internship was a great opportunity, and deep inside I knew that, but I was still uncomfortable knowing I must be around "those" people with a disability. It seemed I still had a way to go in accepting myself. This was obvious since I wasn't ready to accept them.

The staff were not just around to help other people with disabilities, but they wanted to change Syracuse to be more accommodating to anyone handicapped. The staff with disabilities would do things like picket the bus system for wheelchair lifts, bring up a stink about ramps not being in stores, and complain about a lack of wheelchair areas at local sporting arenas. They would march and roll their wheelchairs down city streets, creating traffic jams over things like no accessible bathrooms. I was aghast when they parked their wheelchairs in front of city buses and laid in front of their tires.

I was so embarrassed! I didn't want to participate in any of their radical stunts and tried to distance myself from them. Unfortunately, they got me. They talked me into going with them for free on a train to Washington, D.C. to take in the sites. *Who would not want a free vacation?* I thought. But when I got there, I had to take a subway in the pouring rain with a pack of people with a disability, to have a wet candlelight vigil for the Americans with Disabilities Act. I had to yell things in unison in front of the White House like, "We have rights too" and chants like "We won't go away! We won't go away!" There had to be 1,000 people with disabilities from across the country on Pennsylvania Avenue that evening! Earlier that day, some people flopped out of their wheelchairs and started crawling up the capital's steps. The whole area became a circus!

Why the hell am I with these people? I thought, as rain rolled off my baseball cap brim. I felt miserable and was soaked to my underwear. At the time I had no idea what I was doing was essential to the future of people with disabilities. I also had no idea that this was a steppingstone toward acceptance of myself. But all I knew at the time is I wanted to run away and hide.

I remember a person who worked at Arise, named Kiara. Although Kiara's disability affected her greatly and it was an effort for her to get any words out, I liked her a lot. She was witty, funny, had a charm to herself and was very bold. She was not disabled when you listened to her.

One time, I was "stuck" marching in a St. Patrick's Day parade with her and a bunch of other Arise activists. Kiara always told me *she* wanted to be noticed, and not her wheelchair.

Before the parade, I said, "Kiara, you don't want anyone to notice your wheelchair, right? So, why do you have pink ribbons on it, flashing lights, stickers, and a blast horn? And what's with that huge sign saying, 'disability rights' on the chair's back? That sign is so big you could see it from a blimp."

She smiled and said, "I know, it contradicts my philosophy, huh? But not when you use this philosophy: *sometimes you got to spend money to make money.* In other words, this one time, I want people to draw attention to my chair so they can hear the words coming from it. I'm those words!"

That made me think and was a slight turning point in my self-acceptance. I started listening to people like Kiara with an open mind. By the end of internship, I learned more about myself than what I learned for class.

They are not disabled, WE are disabled, I realized. But being disabled does not mean you can't be independent to the best of your ability. They were not complaining about ramps, accessible bathrooms and wheelchair lifts just to waste time. No, it was much more. They were trying to get the community to allow them to live in it like able-bodied people do.

Another thing I learned: *people with disabilities are not an alien culture to be reckoned with!* We are intelligent, knowledgeable individuals with the same interests, desires, and willingness as able-bodied people. Our only difference is we don't have all the opportunities able bodied people have. Mind you, we are not asking for more opportunities than them, and we're not angry, but we are looking to equal the playing field. By doing this, we can live in perfect harmony.

A lesson learned: *you're only disabled if you let society make you disabled!*

Kiara had a big impact on me. I started to look deeper at a population I always ignored: people with disabilities. Was I steering blind all these years? Was I not paying attention to what was in front of me? I also started to accept myself more and recognize that my only limitations are the ones I put on myself. I found a new community I never knew existed or even thought twice about - *and I was in it!* Until this time, I was so into myself, I had no vision outside of my own issues. In a strange way this internship gave me the perspective I needed to keep moving forward with my life. It also brought me down from that high horse of considering people with disabilities as "other people." I guess when you merge into a community that has a common cause, you don't feel quite so lonely.

During my internship with Arise, Inc., a condition developed in my paralyzed eye. It somehow ulcerated, as my cornea became damaged, and the only way to heal it was to cover it with my eyelid. Tape wasn't working to keep it closed, so an eye surgeon sewed it shut with my own eyelid. In just a few days, my entire eye socket and upper cheek was black and blue.

I was mortified by the appearance of my eye and discolored face, so I insisted on getting a pair of prescription sunglasses. I had them tinted almost black to hide that eye socket. Some of the discoloration peeked around the frames, but I felt a little more confident with the new glasses.

At the same time, my mother talked me into making an old cane our dog chewed on into a "candy cane" for the holiday season. I spray painted the cane white, including the rubber tip, and spiraled red tape down it. I smiled at the finished product.

One exceptionally cold evening in early December, I was walking out of my college class building to my car, wearing my dark glasses, and wobbling with my white-tipped, candy cane.

Clumps of ice dotted the area, and mounds of snirt outlined the parking lot. My car was the only one left in the lot at the time.

A student sat just outside the exit door, reading a book under a frosty streetlamp. As I made my way out the door, carefully placing my cane around the ice patches, he said, "Sir, do you need some help?"

I said, "No, I'm okay. Thanks," then proceeded on my way.

"Be careful," he said. "There's black ice to your right. You sure I can't help you? Where are you trying to go?"

I realized he thought I was blind with my whole getup, so I thought I'd have some fun with it, and temporarily "be blind".

"I'm going to the parking lot," I said, walking with my white tipped cane. I now was exaggerating, tapping my cane side-to-side and swaying my head, all while humming a tune.

"There's nothing over there," the young man said. "Is your ride going to meet you there?"

I ignored him, still swaying my head, and now humming Jingle Bells. I tapped my way forward into the parking lot, heading for my car. Out of the left side of my good eye I noticed the student getting off the bench and staring me down, his jaw dropping open. His curiosity was at its peak; I saw this as my chance.

I tapped my way to my vehicle and purposely fumbled with the keys to unlock the driver's door. I sat in the seat, exchanged my tinted glasses for clear ones, clicked my seatbelt and started the car up. I now glanced in the rear-view mirror and saw the young man walking briskly to my car. He was oblivious to me changing glasses.

At that point I revved my motor up three times, slipped it into gear, spun the vehicle around, and purposely slammed my SUV into a dirty ice bank. I then spun it around the other way and hit a trash can, all the time knowing it would dent my side panel but forfeiting the damage for a good dose of fun. I ended up peeling out of the driveway down the access road, making sure to dart my vehicle side-to-side.

In my rear-view mirror I could see the young man chasing me, yelling for me to stop. I just continued, laughing to myself, and wondering if any security cameras caught me. Perhaps it would be on the local news? I could see the headlines now: "Blind man driving a red SUV, last seen going west on Route 173 in Syracuse. Film at six."

At that point a thought came to me, a warped thought at that, but none-the-less a thought: *Having a disability could actually be fun, if you punctuate people's stereotypes.*

Getting New Gumption

While I was attending OCC, I was able to break away from living at home to renting my own apartment. Of course, I was still a "mama's boy," so I rented a place a short ten-minute drive away from my house. I'd be crazy staying any further away from a home cooked meal, as my only experience at cooking was tossing an animal in a crock-pot, making T.V. dinners, boiling pasta or warming up SpaghettiOs. A microwave became my best friend.

It was so cool to me having the newspaper delivered to my door and having my name/number added to the phone book. My published name was my first claim to fame. Unfortunately, telemarketers also learned my phone number. But I looked forward to those calls. Besides my mother, not many people knew my phone number, so I cherished each phone call I'd get.

One Friday evening I was studying at my apartment when the phone rang. I answered it, "Hello?"

A voice on the phone said, "Hello, is Mr. Mortell there?"

I said in a cheerful voice, "Why yes, I am Mr. Mortell!" I made sure to keep his mispronunciation of my name. "And who do I have the pleasure to speak to?"

The voice said, "My name is Philip, and I..."

"Hey Phillis buddy, how are you today?"

"I'm fine, thank you for asking. I'm from Time Life Cable, and you qualify for…"

I interrupted, "Say Phillis, where you from?"

Philip said, after a brief pause, "That's 'Philip,' and I'm from Time Life Cable…"

I interrupted again, "No-no silly, I mean what land? You know: Burbank, California; Cicero, New York, where? C'mon, talk to me."

"I'm from Kokomo Indiana, and I'd like to tell you, you qualify for…"

"Woo Phillis!" I exclaimed. *"Wooooo dude!!* My papa, he-he's in Kokomo, do you know him? About 5-4, brown eyes, Gemini?"

Philip chuckled, "No Mr. Mortell, I don't. But you qualify for 12 months of…"

I started sniffling, "My pappy, he left me when I was five. Mom said he ran off with the dog groomer. I loved my pappy."

Philip said, "I'm sorry to hear that, Mr. Mortell. But because of being a loyal customer, you qualify for 12 months…

"My pappy, he-he used to sing to me at night. He would sing, really low, *'Oldddd mannn river, that olddd man riverrr'.* Just like that!"

"I see Mr. Mortell." Philip went on, trying to ignore me, "You qualify for an amazing offer of twelve months…"

"Say, Phillis, can you do me a favor? Could you sing a bit for me, just like my pappy? It would mean a whole lot to me. Then I'll listen to your amazing offer."

Philip shot in, with flat intonation, "I really can't Mr. Mortell. Let me offer you twelve months of…"

"C'mon Phillis," I whined. "I'll start: *Olddd mannn river, that old man—*" I stopped. "Phillis, you're, you're not singing. Why is that? It hurts me so."

He started to plead, "Mr. Mortell, I really can't."

"Okay, tell you what, you do it solo then, just one line. On three…ready? One, two, three."

To my surprise, Philip sang quietly, in a low tone, *"Olddd mannn river,"* then abruptly ended.

I again sniffed, "Phillis, you sound just like my pappy." I then brightened up. "You are, *you ARE my pappy*!! I finally found you!"

Philip said, "I'm not your father."

I then said, very loud and in a raspy voice, "Then, who's your daddy? ME! Yes, I'm your ***daddyyyyy!!***"

It took Phil that long to finally hang up.

• • •

I graduated from Onondaga Community College with an associate degree in Human Services. I never dreamt I could do this - in fact, I was told it was impossible, given the extent of my brain injury. For the first time since the car accident, I had an identity. I was more than just a brain damaged statistic. I was an intelligent, community citizen who happened to have a brain injury. That two-year degree became the turning point in finding out who I was. There was a diploma on the wall reading *Steven Martell, Associates Degree in Human Services*. I earned the degree, and no one helped me get it. I went from not being able to write a five-paragraph essay to securing a full two-year diploma.

I felt as if society approved of me again, but this time, in a different way. I didn't have to play music, sing, or do a comedy routine to have society's approval. I felt as if society came to me because of what I had, not what I did to entertain them.

Shortly after I graduated, my advisor from Onondaga Community College requested to meet with me, one last time before I left school and hung up my hat on education. He knew I was lost as to what direction I was going to take now. However, upon graduation Arise hired me for two hours a week to monitor a traumatic brain injury support group. That involved keeping the group going and not let it stall to silence. The payment was just a stipend, so I did not earn enough to jeopardize my Social Security payments. This stipend did help me find some meaning in life, but my curiosity as to why my advisor wanted to see me got me really nervous. Was he going to say they made a mistake in calculating grades and I really did not graduate? Would I have to quit the job?? Wacky but troubling hypothetical situations entered my mind.

As I sat alone in my advisor's office, it felt as if I was waiting in the hospital room for Dr. Jimkee, who would soon ruin my dreams. My body was tense. I passed time tapping my fingers on the table and reading motivational posters taped up all over the room.

My adviser finally walked in and hung up his windbreaker, smiling. "Steve, thanks for coming in." He sat down; I shined an animated grin.

"Steve, we got to talk." My grin flat lined. "You didn't just squeak by to graduate. You earned a solid 3.5 GPA. I bet with your sure determination you could get a BA degree. "

I now flashed a genuine smile. "Really?"

My advisor nodded. "But be aware, the intensity will be ramped up, though. You may consider taking the next two years of college over three or four years. You don't want to overwhelm yourself."

I relaxed as I was fearing the worse from him. But there it was again - that phrase - "don't overwhelm yourself." Well, I had heard that before. I knew what it meant, but it had less meaning hearing it now then years before. I just demonstrated I could prove the doctor's wrong, didn't I? I still didn't think I would ever work more than 2 hours a week, but I now knew I was capable of so much more than anyone previously thought.

After much research, I decided to pursue my BA degree in psychology. The big problem was that I had no idea how I was going to pay for it, or if I could even pass the courses, for that matter. I heeded the ominous warning from my past advisor to take it slow, and honestly, my confidence was pushed back a little. I was intimidated by a bigger school and the bar being raised higher.

Despite my hesitation about trying to get my BA degree, I snooped around to see what funding I could get. I knew there were special programs for people with disabilities, but I didn't realize how many existed, if you did some investigation. One was state vocational rehabilitation. After researching it, the program looked good, so I applied for it.

This program varies by state, and might be called something different in your state, but here in Syracuse, NY, it was called Vocational Educational Services for Individuals with Disabilities (or VESID). I was appointed to Patricia, a vocational rehabilitation counselor.

I explained to Patricia what my last advisor said, suggesting I pace myself. However, she told me about Columbia College, which is in Missouri but had an extension site at the 174th Tactical Fighter Wing in Mattydale, NY. The extension site was for enlisted personnel, but civilians were welcome to the school, providing there was space after military people enrolled. The curriculum required longer school hours with the semesters cut in half. However, they advised students to take only two classes a semester, which translates to full time, or the equivalent of taking four classes during a regular semester.

Patricia suggested I try Columbia College and if it were too much for me, we would cut back. She was not "gloom and doom" like the doctors; she was realistic. The difference was she had a back-up plan to aim towards success, where the doctors didn't.

The 174th Tactical Fighter Wing was only about eight miles from my home, so I enrolled in Columbia College and rolled over whatever credits I could from OCC. As Patricia said, the classes were twice as long, but the arrangement was compatible to my disability. This class structure gave me more time to focus on studying. Although it was difficult to keep up my lessons with the fatigue that hit me, fewer classes gave me the freedom to find the best way to pace myself.

This plan worked out well, and I was able to find a winning pace to minimize the fatigue factor while honoring my academic responsibilities. But the lessons I learned were not held in traditional college classrooms. The classrooms were the Airforce training facilities on the base, which was kind of cool, as gas masks hung on the walls in some of them. I remember studying the different shapes and sizes of them, not realizing there was such a variety of designer gas masks to choose from! I picked out my favorite one to grab in case of a mustard gas attack.

All went well until the Gulf War broke out. The planes left the hangers, and our gas mask rooms were closed to us. Apparently, they held "secret" military operations in the rooms, and us students were not invited to them anymore. An unheated empty hanger then became our classroom, as rows of chairs lined the colossal garage. Mattydale almost borders Syracuse, so it is known for cold winters, and sitting in a hanger in January was no exception. My note taker insisted she had to use a pencil because the frigid cold would make ink in her pen gummy up.

I would go to class wearing a snorkel jacket and gloves, with a thermos of hot chocolate. Sometimes I would model a ski mask. Several evenings it would drop to five below zero, in which my body would "seize-up" from the cold, despite my thermal underwear. This caused my frail body to contract and become a solid rock. During a frigid cold spell for one week, I had to have two classmates carry me out to my car and toss me in my front seat. There I would sit in the fetal position until the heater would thaw me out and my limbs would start to emerge. I felt like I was breaking out of a cocoon.

As I was warned, the academics were more trying, and it was harder for me to concentrate or recall information. I tried unusual ways to study in attempt to skirt the residual effects of my brain injury. Sometimes, I would try to "force" myself to memorize a lesson. This did not work, as it just intensified confusion in my marred memory. But although I knew I became confused with a given lesson, sometimes I could not recall *why* I became confused to begin with. So, I would trick myself. In a roundabout way, sometimes revisiting the source of the confusion would help me understand the lesson, as now my perspective of it could be different. Say, this is a bit radical and may not work for everyone, but it did for me.

A more common technique I used is "repetition," but I would modify it. In an absurd kind of way, my brain injury became a benefit! Check this out, I would repeat the passage or lesson I was to remember. After I thought I remembered it, I would purposely do something to forget it (kind of easy to do with my brain injury). I don't know, watch a quarter of a football game, make a grilled cheese sandwich, do a crossword puzzle, some monumental event to distract myself. Then I would return to what I tried to forget and memorize it again. In the future, I would recall the event that distracted me after learning it, and many times I could recall the lesson.

A variation of repetition is actually helping me write this book! I write a few paragraphs, walk away, and eat a peanut butter sandwich, then return to the book. Guess what, I forgot what

I wrote! So, to me, I'm reading something new, which makes it easier to notice grammatical mistakes. It's easier to catch someone else's writing blunders, even if they're your own.

A classic I use even today is "word association", usually for events or names. An example: pretend I must get on a bus at 4:00. I would remember a bus has four tires, which tips me off to the time. Another example is if someone is named "Sandy Sonny," I would remember her name as a sunny beach, as a "sonny beach" is "sandy." I find it easier to remember familiar terms then to recall uncharted names.

My wayward thinking and combination of memory techniques worked out: I graduated from Columbia College with a Bachelor of Science in Psychology, and my final GPA was 3.8. My motivation was over the top! Not only did this degree look great on my resume, but I also felt more defined as a person.

I remember Norm looking at my degree and shaking his head. He said, "Steve Martell with a psychology degree. Boy, that's dangerous!" Norm could have been joking, but for some reason, I believed he was serious. His narcissistic personality was sounding loud.

Norm moved back to Brewerton as he never made it big as a Boston musician. I'm not sure if he was jealous of me getting a bachelor's degree or if he was trying to be sarcastic. Perhaps he was miffed because he had a genius I.Q. and should be where I am. Either way, he returned to the Syracuse area homeless and a full-fledged alcoholic.

I tried to help Norm with the same programs that helped me, but I believe he thought he was better than what the programs had to offer. He never said it, but I could see it in his eyes. Norm snubbed my attempts to help him; he would not see substance abuse as a disability, or a social disease.

I got Norm off the street and let him make a bedroom in my apartment's walk-in closet. Sadly, I had to ask him to leave when I learned he was stealing from me to buy booze. But Elliott and I still tried to help Norm as he lived in the Rescue Mission. Unwittingly, Norm taught me a valuable lesson, one I could never learn in college: *to reach higher ground you can't surrender to your fractured dreams and call life quits. Make new, achievable dreams.*

Overall, the school experience, both OCC and Columbia College, was the hardest, but the best thing I did for myself after the accident. While I was in school, I found myself being in the same boat as other students who leaned on each other for support. It was a good feeling that some students looked towards me for support and paid no attention to my handicap.

My personality and sense of humor was steadily coming back. I became proud of who I was. Entertaining people was now falling to the background and a new, more realistic image was emerging from me! And, most importantly, the words

Hazel said were fading in my mind, especially as some friend-ships blossomed into girlfriends and dating!

Just before graduation from Columbia College, a psychology professor told me that a Bachelor's of Arts in Psychology does not make you a psychologist. Basically, it sets the foundation for getting a master's degree in a career. I had no thought whatsoever about getting a master's degree. Not only was it farfetched for me to even consider reaching that level of academic achievement, economically there was no way I could even swing the tuition. I surrendered to the idea that I was to be on fixed income all my life and work my two-hour a week stipend gig. The very fact that I could go as far as I did in education was more than anyone, including me, could fathom. But I wondered if I could do any paid employment above my stipend and still get my monthly SSD benefits? That would be awesome if I could!

Well, sometimes "awesome" works out. I learned from Sophia, a head injury support member, that because she was on SSD, the national rules were she could work and earn an unlimited amount of income for up to 9 months (called a 9-month Trial Work Period) and it would not affect her monthly benefits. After the 9th month, if she worked and earned under a certain amount every month (called Substantial Gainful Activity or SGA) she could keep all her SSD monthly benefits *and* her earned income. Sophia said if her earnings went over the SGA, she chanced losing her monthly benefits and would live off her earnings.

"I work part time in customer service," she said, "so I'm not earning over the SGA. It's all good."

I found Sophia's information intriguing, so kept it in the back of my head.

I continued my 2-hour-a-week job at Arise, which I looked forward to every Tuesday. I found it kind of fun and a bit challenging. The support group fluctuated between 4 to 8 people, all who had a brain injury like me. A few other faithful members were a young survivor of a stroke and another who survived Reye's Syndrome, a rare swelling of the brain. In any event, all had a closed head injury.

My group facilitation was most successful if I could create a non-threatening atmosphere and encourage people to champion each other. Eventually, the group would run itself. Members would help each other mentally, spiritually and trade information about community integration despite their disability.

Most of my group facilitation techniques I learned in college, even taking one class at OCC that was solely geared towards group counseling. Although I put entertaining on the back burner, I couldn't help but to inject humor, which lightened the setting and helped the group flow. I found eventually others would inject a bit of humor. I laughed with them.

Sometimes I would share community job leads with the group. Jokingly, a member asked if I had any jobs to be an astronaut for NASA. I told him I was sorry, but I just filled my last NASA job, but would he settle on being a test pilot for a F-22 Raptor?

This comeback was not the ultimate knee slapper, but for a mixed crowd, it seemed appropriate. Everyone had a little chuckle, and at the same time I noticed the director of Arise observing the group, smiling.

A few weeks later, after monitoring a support group, the director of Arise stopped me just before I walked out the door.

"Steve," he said, "looks like you're doing a nice job with the TBI group. I got some good vibes coming from it!"

I smiled, "Thanks. I like to think my two-hour paycheck is worth every penny."

"Actually, that's exactly what I want to talk to you about." The director then invited me into his office. I sat down.

"Everyone here on staff likes the work you're doing," the director said, "including me. You have your bachelor's in psychology, and it shows. You seem to get through to all the consumers here. They listen to you. So, I'm going to toss this right out to you: *would you like to come on staff to be a per diem peer counselor?* Ellie would be your supervisor and your time would flex no more than 10 and 15 hours a week, so you work as needed. We need a person to meet new referrals who are disabled and explain to them about our services. Your 'customer service' expertise and the way you put people to ease would be a *perfect* fit for this position!"

I dropped my jaw and pointed at my chest, "What? Are you talking to me?"

He looked at both sides of his office then grinned, "You're the only one here!"

I was speechless. I was out of words. In fact, my mind went totally blank. I think the director could sense my shock.

"Look Steve," he said, "you don't have to answer now. Think about it. But I tell you, it would be great to get you on the team! We could start you at $2.50 an hour, no benefits, but I know you get Medicare. I need to know in a few days; I need to know by this Friday."

I was most mesmerized because this per diem job offer came to me, I did not pursue the offer. So now, someone actually saw and liked my work ability! I recalled the doctors saying I could never work, but somehow, I went from working 2 hours a week to being asked to work up to 15 hours a week.

Still, I was very apprehensive about losing my monthly $480.00 SSD check because of working. I mean, that was the only thing I had to live on. I figured it out on a calculator: if I had to live just on my per diem earnings because I lost SSD, at $2.50 an hour, times a max of 15 hours a week, times 4 weeks a month, I would only take home $150 a month…and that's *before* taxes! I can't live on $150 a month!! I started to hyperventilate at the very thought.

I wanted a second opinion, so I grabbed a different calculator. It came out to the same figure. The only difference was the font of the numbers.

I lazily tossed the calculator to my side and rolled my eyes. *How does anyone get off from the system and become self-sufficient?* I thought. *I guess if you get on SSD, you die on SSD.*

I then faintly recalled Sophia from my support group telling me how she can work and still collect her full SSD, if she didn't go over the SGA. This was too good to be true; I thought she had to be a special case. So, a few days later I talked to a Social Security representative. To my surprise it was true, and for everyone collecting SSD, not just her. Even more in my favor, that particular year the Social Security Administration only counted earnings over $200.00 as a TWP month, and I'm only grossing $150 a month. I would keep my $150.00 pay plus $480.00 monthly benefits, while saving my TWP months! Say, I still may not live high on the horse with a total of $630.00 a month to live on, but it beats just $150 a month!

Here's the important piece: my support group was working for members. Now here's the ironic piece: the support group was working for *me!* Just because I was the moderator didn't mean I was "above" other people or not a member. No, just the opposite. I got knowledge and insight from listening to other people with a traumatic brain injury. Selfishly, sometimes I brought up subjects that I wanted to know more about and valued the way other people handled situations. These situations were unique to our culture. And, of course, Sophia gave me knowledge that would help change the course of my life!

I gladly accepted the job offer from the director. From the positive response I got from TBI group members and Arise staff, I felt confident with my abilities. From the discussion I had with the Social Security Administration, I felt relieved knowing I would not mess up my SSD benefits. All the stars lined up to make this a "win-win" situation. What I wasn't sure about was if I could stay awake long enough to work up to 15 hours a week. For me, working this job and the increase of hours were uncharted waters.

Through trial and error, I learned I had to rest before and after I worked. Fortunately, this job was not hard to learn or do, so it was easy on my mind. It didn't involve much writing either, which was a God send, because I had no note taker.

Also, I learned to work about three hours a day I was going to have to stretch my body. Not doing this would cause my body to "seize up" and I would start walking like Frankenstein. In part these stretches involved me getting on the floor and leaning backwards to stretch my back, with my legs bent under my keester. I looked like a human switchblade.

I still have to work on physical therapy to this day. Basically, I move around and try to activate inactive muscles that would restrict me from walking or even lifting simple objects, like a pen. I do this first thing in the morning every day of my life. If I miss even one day I can hardly walk or function at all. Aerobic exercise helps keep my blood circulating, increases my stamina, and reduces health risks. This exercise routine allows me to function and without doing it daily, my body would decline rapidly.

I found an empty out-of-site room at Arise to do my physical therapy in, preventing a spectacle of stretching in public. This worked out fine, until one day they decided to make the room a "rental closet" for health accessories, like wheelchairs and shower seats. I resumed my search for a private spot to stretch out. The only place I could find was the oversized toilet stall in a lady's room. The two stalls in the bathroom were so wide, two wheelchairs could navigate in each. A bathroom floor is not the most appealing place to do stretching exercises, but it sure beats an open parking lot. Fortunately, this room was "out-of-order," so no one used it.

One Monday morning, I missed my stretching at home, so I decided to do it in the lady's room toilet stall. I closed the metal door to give me full floor space, dropped to my knees, then stretched backwards. I ignored the fact the "out-of-order" sign was missing, and someone fixed the plumbing over the weekend.

As I laid on the floor with my legs tucked under me and arching my back, I heard the door open and the sound of foot-steps. This got my attention. Then, the stall door next to me closed, and I saw through the bottom crack of the stall a pair of high heel shoes…then a pair of underwear fall on the shoes… then a slip fall on the underwear…then a dress fall on the slip, and then… "a noise".

I froze in my spot, not uttering a sound, kind of like a deer in headlights. Just then, I heard another set of footsteps, but by then the first lady finished her business, so the second set of high heels took her place. Right behind the high heels I heard a quiet rolling sound, and under the bathroom stall I saw two wheels from a wheelchair stop in front of my door. I now froze even stiffer than I already was.

After thirty seconds of me staying motionless on the floor, a lady's voice said, "Excuse me, are you okay? Will you be much longer?"

I had no idea what to do, so I said in my highest, squeak-iest voice, "Well, I'm really not feeling well. It may be a while."

Just then, the toilet next to my stall flushed, and the lady exited the stall. The woman in the wheelchair took her place.

I was still arched back with my legs tucked under me, when the lady in the wheelchair completed her mission, washed her hands, and rolled out.

The room was now silent; I exhaled a sigh of relief. I got up from my horizontal position, stood on my feet, and slowly opened the metal stall door. I looked both ways. When I saw myself clear, I briskly walked to the door, my cane clunking in stride, now knowing I was free. As I reached for the door handle, the door suddenly opened, and another woman walked in. When she saw me, she widened her eyes and exclaimed, "OH!," obviously shocked.

I then motioned back to the bathroom stalls, and I said in a flat, slow tone, "It's okay ma'am I just fixed the toilets. But you may want to use stall number one, the floor seems to be cleaner."

I was fortunate not to get fired from the bathroom fiasco, because I needed this job. This per diem position helped me feel good about myself. Not only did I continue to lead the head injury support group, and explained Arise services to new referrals, but I found myself peer counseling one-to-one with individuals. Often, I would talk to people regarding issues coping with their disability, no matter what it was. I even worked some weekends, taking them to art therapy with Suzanne Masters, a friend of mine who is an art therapist.

This little job made me puff my chest out, but the ultimate compliment was from Joanne, a head injury survivor. She said, "Steve, I like you. You don't talk to me like one of the doctors or psychologists, you talk to me like a 'real person.' Actually, I feel like a real person around you."

Well, I broke the news to Joanne that she was a "real person," none-the-less her testimony did humble me. But what her statement also did was verify that I wasn't just imagining things. She confirmed my thoughts that some clinicians are only trained to help you survive, but many lacked the knowledge to help you *live*. "Living" could only come from your soul, the same area that gives you unprecedented self-drive.

I was working at Arise, Inc. for about six months when I met a student from Syracuse University, better known as SU. She was doing an internship at Arise. This person was pursuing a master's degree in Vocational Rehabilitation Counseling. I used to joke about how bad the job market would have to be to get a master's degree in "working," because "working" in a job that requires a degree to "work" makes about as much sense as buying "dehydrated water" or sweeping a dirt driveway. But she explained to drop the name "vocational," as it was misleading, and keep the "rehabilitation counseling" part. It's psychosocial counseling, or rather helping people with disabilities to live a productive life, in this case.

It then occurred to me that my VESID counselor had that same degree and she helped me immensely. I was sold; I was going to try my best to get a degree in Vocational Rehabilitation Counseling. *What could be sweeter then to become the person that helped you?* With that concept, I decided to apply to SU. *What would it hurt?* I thought. *It looks like I can do anything I want!* I started to get cocky. But was I getting overconfident??

Well, reality hit me: I was not allowed into SU. I thought I did everything right and jumped through all their hoops to be accepted, but still my efforts fell short. I had a BA in Psychology with a GPA of 3.8, good enough average to get into the program. I know having a disability did not preclude me from program entrance, but I believe it was because of my specific disability: a brain injury. This was not just a "head injury," mind you, as I see a head injury as a bad hair day. No, this was much more. It was full blown, 100%, whole wheat, nothing added, brain damage!

No one from SU told me they would not let me in because of my brain injury, but I sensed it from the get-go. I don't think it was paranoia. One of the requirements was I had to write a 1,500-word entrance essay with the admission test. Although I passed the test, I included information about my brain injury in the essay. *Was this a mistake?* I thought. I regret writing about it and believe I released too much personal information. My theory was if people knew I got a bachelor's degree with brain trauma, then it would make me look better, almost as if I was a celebrity! This obviously was a false assumption and a grave miscalculation on my part.

I hit my forehead with my right hand and said to myself, "Stupid, stupid! What was I thinking?" Now, getting accepted into SU became an obsession, a personal quest, just so I could prove I could do it.

I applied again, and I was denied again. *Why is this?* I asked myself. *You only have to have a 3.5 GPA to get in and my 3.8 GPA was more than sufficient.* So, I met with the school dean of Vocational Rehabilitation Counseling to find out why I was declined. He never gave me a direct answer, but finally said if I got a recommendation from a past psychology professor, then they would consider accepting me. So, I got a recommendation from a psychology teacher from Columbia College.

Finally, after weeks of sweat and toil, I got an acceptance letter to enter the Vocational Rehabilitation Counseling program at SU. But I didn't know if they felt I was a viable candidate or if I was just a pain in the rear, an irritating pest to shut up.

"Accept the guy, already." I could hear the administrators say. "That would shut him up. God, he's as annoying as one of my whining kids!"

So now I could pursue my Masters. But how was I going to pay for it all? I looked into VESID, only to find out they could pay for just three credit hours. The tuition was astronomically high. I qualified for a small school scholarship, which helped, but still a large amount was outstanding.

Arise again came to my rescue. A staff member told me about a rarely used work incentive built into Social Security, called a PASS (Plan for Achieving Self Support). It allowed me to collect the full amount of Supplementary Security Income (SSI) and all my SSD. Without a PASS, one cannot get SSD and SSI. The PASS waivers this rule.

I could use SSI for living expenses and SSD would pay for college tuition, as long as I had a vocational goal. I did have one: becoming a Vocational Rehabilitation Counselor, like Patricia. If I found out getting a master's degree was too much to take, then the PASS would stop, I would cease getting SSI, and I would return to SSD for my living expense. So really, there was no risk. I resigned from Arise to attend school, but the director told me I was welcome back any time. That was a comfort. But now reality hit me: I was accepted into a master's degree program at a major university! I became nervous beyond belief.

The Sunday evening before I was going to start my crusade at SU, I sat alone in my apartment, lights turned down low, sipping on some fine bourbon.

I looked straight and focused my eyes on nothing. *Am I doing too much?* I thought to myself. *Am I pressing the bar too far?*

I took another taste from my glass and looked at a paper with my upcoming courses. I raised it to my face and started reading, just as I did one glass of bourbon ago: *Intro to Rehabilitation Counseling; Psychosocial Aspects of Disability; Advanced Statistics; The Psychological Anatomy of the Brain.* I noted the course agenda on the paper was the same as three minutes earlier; nothing disappeared.

I frowned then tossed the paper to the side, "I can't do this," I whispered, then took a quick swig of whisky and slammed the glass on the table. *"Who the hell am I kidding?"*

I yelled in open air, ***"I can't do this!!"*** I sobbed, then continued talking to myself, shaking a low hanging head. "I can't do this God. I'm sorry Dad."

I raised my head and sniffed, talking to the air again, "Dad, this is the big league and I have no business running with the big dogs. Should I just call SU and pull out before it's too late?"

I thought a few seconds, *well, I guess my father did tell me to have faith.* I paused, then slowly limped over to my stereo. I tossed my cane down and plopped down in a chair next to it, then lazily fingered through my albums, until I found a record from Cheap Trick. I put it on the record player post and played the track, "Surrender." I then leaned back, closed my eyes, and dozed off.

• • •

I did show up for my first day of college, albeit a bit tired from my private "pity party" the evening before. But I admit I looked for the nearest exit, preparing to forever leave. As I sat in the front row so I could hear the instructor, classmates filed into the seats behind me. I was nervous, still wondering if I belonged in that room with "super smart people."

The instructor then walked into the room wearing a tall Dr. Seuss hat. Out came a trickle of laughter from the room. I forced a nervous smile, not knowing what to expect or what was going on. He then opened the Dr. Seuss book, "Oh the Places You'll Go!" and started to recite from it:

> "You have brains in your head.
> You have feet in your shoes.
> You can steer yourself any
> direction you choose. You're
> on your own. And you know
> what you know. And YOU are
> the one who'll decide where to
> go."

(Dr. Seuss, "Oh, the Places you'll Go!" Random House 1990)

The instructor closed the Dr. Seuss book and raised it in the air. "This is the only book you need in this class," he said. "This is the only book you need in *any* class. And these are the only words you need from any book." He set it on the podium in front of him. "You all came this far, so you guys are no stooges. It's up to all of you to decide your future. Now, when you all graduate and have a new set of tools, it's up to you to decide where to go."

The words he said made me stop and think, and they were the exact words I needed at the time. He and Dr. Seuss where exactly right: I am in control of my destiny. No one else can be blamed for my failure and no one else could be praised for my achievements. But the most comforting word he said was "when" you graduate, not "if" you graduate. So, I decided to stay for the rest of the class and see how it played out.

This first class was a real struggle. Although I thought I was polished at writing, my Professor, Paul Salomone, who was also my advisor, was the former editor of a psychological magazine and had me write my first paper five times until I got it right. I felt like I was in EOC again! I was ready to quit to the disdain of Dr. Seuss. But Professor Salomone talked me into staying, stressing my success in academics so far. I decided to give it one last whirl. The thing is all my life I gave my education "one last whirl" and it still worked out. But Syracuse University was a different animal, a different playing field.

I made friends with other students in the program, Bea, Amy, and Don, who helped me navigate the big campus and who would take my notes with carbon paper. I got hooked up with a school counselor who catered to people with special needs. My apartment looked like a papermill, as stacks of scholastic periodicals outlined my bed. My floor looked like a library drop box. I had to go "full force" to attack school and felt I had to "overcompensate" to stay ahead.

With supports in hand, I managed to pass all four classes my first semester, brandishing one with a B, two with an A- and a third with an A! This success propelled me to want to do even better. I was required to practice my skills in the community, so I did internships at OCM BOCES, North Syracuse Junior High and the Syracuse Veteran's Administration Hospital.

It was more important than ever to pace myself, especially at the master's level. So, instead of taking a full course load every spring and fall semester, I also took a class during the summer. The whole idea I had was to elongate the classes as to not overwhelm myself. I didn't want to sound like one of the doctors, but it was true.

One class I took over the summer was called Cross Cultural Counseling. This course was an elective offered during the summer when most students were at home, so many students were absent from campus. It was sponsored in part by The League of Foreign Students.

The ironic part is I was the only American student in the class. The rest of it was made up by students from other countries, like China, Pakistan, Indonesia, and India. Because it was a perfect mix of people from different countries and seeing how the teacher was the only one from Kenya, it was decided that the last day of class, everyone would bring in a dish from their native country and share it.

Not blaming my head injury for forgetting, but I noticed on my calendar I was to bring in American food that last class… *and the last class was this very day!!* I only had four hours until it started. I swallowed hard and had nothing prepared.

I opened a cupboard: nothing. Then another: just SpaghettiOs. The refrigerator: only Yoohoo. But my freezer was packed full of my favorite quick meal: Banquet Chicken T.V. dinners, complete, with apple crumb for dessert. I took out seven of them, removed the film, then put them on every rack in the preheated oven at 350.

Twenty-five minutes later, I took them out. I put the chicken in a small cooler, then all the peas, mash potatoes and apple crisp in plastic containers. I then sped down the road with the vittles in the back seat, kind of like a caterer trying to meet his deadline.

I arrived at class and people were just setting out their food on the table. I set mine on the table when someone with broken English said, "Oh, that smells good!" He handed me a marker and paper. "Please write down what country it comes from and any history behind it and place it in front of your food."

With a flat smile and tight lips, I said, "Ah, no problem. I'm all over that." This was a very awkward moment, to say the least. I hoped I wouldn't burn in hell for doing what I was about to do.

I took the marker and paper, then wrote down: *"Fine American Cuisine."* I thought for a second, then continued writing. *"Chicken Martelli, with savory peas and fresh Apple Cobbler. A family recipe originally created by my great-great-great grandfather, Captain Bo Martelli, after the War of 1812."*

My food was a hit! People gobbled it down like no tomorrow. The compliments just kept on coming, and I explained how I spent the entire weekend slaving over a hot stove to prepare it.

One person came up to me while eating a chicken leg, "Mr. Martell," he said, "this is the best chicken I ever had! Can I have your secret?"

I had to think up a quick lie. "Ah, sorry, I promised my family I'd never release the secret, even turning down $50,000 from Banquet Chicken for it. Let's just say it all depends on what you feed the birds."

• • •

Two years later, I graduated from Syracuse University with a dual Master of Science degree in Rehabilitation Counseling and Counselor Education with a 3.8 GPA. To further that, I passed my Certified Rehabilitation Counselor (CRC) exam, a grueling 7-hour exam, but my special needs counselor let me break it up over the course of two days. Students without this accommodation had only one day to do it. It is comparable to a board exam for all rehabilitation counselors. I was so mentally drained that after day two of it I could only stare mindlessly at a wall.

The Syracuse Sunday Herald American did a front page, three-page story about me graduating from Syracuse University with a dual master's degree, despite having a severe brain injury. My phone was always ringing, not from telemarketers, but from people congratulating me!

One of the best things that came out of my graduation was a party for me that was held at a local banquet hall. My mother, hardly able to walk now because of multiple health problems, came to it and sat at the head table with the bouquet of roses I got her. The proud glow on her face knowing what I accomplished in my life with the hurdles I had to jump over was the most precious and heartwarming thing I ever experienced.

What I Learned

Now let me talk more about the programs that helped me get through school, and how I found them. The most important thing I did for myself was to keep talking to people. Notice that I keep saying that so-and-so told me about this program or that one. Even in today's world of Google, word of mouth is still our best bet. Keep talking to people "in the know" and who have taken a path similar to yours to find the best opportunities. Join a support group! I know they work.

As mentioned before, VESID helped me a great deal. Now in New York State it's called Adult Career and Continuing Education Services-Vocational Rehabilitation (ACCES-VR), or a completely different name, depending on your state of residence. In any event it's considered state vocational rehabilitation. All of these programs help people with disabilities get a job or sponsor them to go to school. Any financial benefits they could sponsor you with depends on many factors, but you'll never know if they can help until you ask. After they financially help students, they may be able to give them job leads.

I also had tuition assistance to help me get through college. New York State helps low-income students with college through TAP, while the federal government offers help via PELL. That money was used up through OCC and Columbia College, so SU had to be bought another way. Again, I heard about grants through a friend. I did the research and took the time to apply to different scholarships, finally snagging one.

The thing is you have to decide what career you want to pursue and forge ahead. This is not as important when pursuing an associate degree, but it becomes an issue when pursuing a bachelors and especially a master's degree. If you want to reach a career but don't know what it is yet, then state vocational rehabilitation could help with that, too. Perhaps taking a vocational assessment could help. They have, oh so many tools for vocational discovery!

Now let's talk about my attitude to pursue post-grad education. I had plenty of excuses to not pursue school, didn't I? But I opened my mind to alternatives and started thinking in the abstract, and that helped drive my quest forward. When I got to Syracuse University, I could have stopped because my thought was that I couldn't pay for it. Guess what, that was an excuse! I took the time I needed to confront that excuse, and you can too, if you zero-in on an end goal and you're stubborn, like me!

I previously explained PASS, which paid for much of my tuition at Syracuse University. I also mentioned the program is rarely used because the application is a pain in the drain! Heck, it's similar to making a business plan. In my case I had to outline my college career, create a detailed plan, even make a specific time schedule. I had to convince and prove to SSA staff the program was feasible. Still, even some SSA representatives thought I could not do it. Let me go further on this subject.

When I wrote my PASS, there was little help. I truly was shooting from the hip. I had to modify it, justify it, amend it, and re-calculate my figures a good ten times before it was accepted. Today, there are people who help develop a PASS; there's even an office dedicated to it. But there will always be surprise "halts" or challenges that come up that seem to be a roadblock. Yes, those big, fat "no's." That's when you smile and curve your plan, so they become a "yes."

Think about writing a PASS as getting a job. You apply, then apply again, get an interview, hear "no," then go apply for another job. Maybe apply for the same job in a few months. You keep going until you hear a "yes." "No" is never an answer. It may be for that particular gig, but it's not the end of the line. *Never let "NO" stop you from pursuing your dreams!* I know, this is the most used wisdom since some caveman had a square wheel and dreamt of a round one. But I bet someone told him the round wheel would never work. Dreaming is how society progresses.

These programs worked for me but may not work for everyone. It's the same thing in reverse. Some things might work for you, but not me. It all depends on your willingness, the fire in your gut, the spit in your eye, and your persistence level. Oh yes, and your attitude. As far as your background goes, your race or your family situation—all I can say is, disability knows no color, no culture, political affiliation, gender, or background. It's you against the world baby, or you with the world, depending on if you see the glass half empty or half full. But hey, it's still the same glass; *it's up to you to decide how high to fill it.* Just ask Dr. Seuss.

Another point to mention is your "self-talk." Sometimes people put words in your head you'd rather not say, but sometimes, you still say them. "Where did that come from?" you may ask yourself. Let me explain this one.

I remember telling myself that I couldn't do things because I was told I couldn't. I was told I would never work again, that I would always be nothing, nada, zippo. I let myself believe that for *wayyyy* too long. But I finally emerged from my systemic depression when I decided to do things for myself. I would challenge myself to see what I could be. So, if your self-talk is telling you, "I can't," if that devil on your shoulder is slapping your face, slap that devil back and turn the "cant's into "cans." This may sound like a cliché, but in the context of this book, it comes from a unique perspective.

You can also throw out negative vibes you get from society, or at least you think you get from society. What I mean is, I used to think I couldn't do certain things because we were poor, especially after my father passed away. I thought I'd never go to college because it was reserved for the elite. Well, now I know that's all hogwash! I had to fight, scrounge, and swallow my pride for every penny I could get to go to school. I had to eat cheap peanut butter and shop at the thrift store. No, I didn't have lobster and caviar every night, but you know what? My needs were met. My needs were met to complete my current adventure, then go on to my next one, because I had a vision and refused to look back.

CHAPTER VIII

STILL BUILDING: MORE RESOURCES FOR SUCCESS

Despite all my education, I could not get a job. Months went by, and after over 100 resumes, cover letters and applications sent, I had only been interviewed a few times. When I was interviewed, I always seemed to be the "first runner up" and then told, "but the person that hires you is a lucky person!"

"C'mon," I would mumble to myself after reading another rejection letter, "you could be that lucky person."

Were employers ganging up on me? I started wondering why I even applied for jobs in the first place. The callback never came. I was totally at a loss as to what to do; confused and dismayed.

I went back to Patricia at VESID with my tail between my legs, and she told me about an upstart employment agency called, "Supports Unlimited." This agency was funded by a grant under a well-known, not-for-profit sheltered workshop called Consolidated Industries, and they needed part-time job coaches. A job coach showed individuals with a disability how to do a job at a business, then stepped back when the person could do the job independently. First, the job coach would learn how to do the job and then teach the newly acquired skills to the person with a disability.

Even though I had this interesting opportunity, I still felt defeated. I could get a part-time job anywhere, with Arise as proof, but the reason I plugged on through college is so I could get a full-time job and become self-supporting. Subconsciously I still had that "meter man" and "meteorologist" rational from way back when, wanting a career and *not* just a job!

Depression threatened to creep back in, because I convinced myself that people were wary of hiring someone with a brain injury. I didn't emphasize my disability on my resume, but I still felt like people could "see it" somehow. I shrugged it all off, though, and interviewed with Vicky, the coordinator of Supports Unlimited, and her assistant, Kate. Sure, I didn't think

I would get it, but what was one more interview? I could just add it to the junk pile of rejection letters.

I sat in the lobby of Supports Unlimited 10 minutes before the interview and finished a paper application. I found this as a suitable time to take a nap. I slouched in my chair, kind of like an old man slipping out of his seat and dozed off. Kate walked up to me as I sawed wood with my mouth wide open.

"Steve," she softly said, gently rocking me. I still snored away. Kate shook me a bit harsher and talked louder, "*Mr. Martell...*"

I gasped and opened my eyes. I looked at her, a bit discombobulated, "Huh?"

She puckered her lips and shook her head. "I hate to wake you, but it's time for your interview. You are awake, right?"

"Me?" I slowly stood up by pushing up with my cane, "Sharp as a tack here! Lead on." I followed Kate to a room, where Vicky waited.

That job interview was one of the easiest I did. Why? Because my heart just wasn't into it. I was so cavalier with the interview I didn't care if I got the job or not. I don't even remember showering for it! My hair was a mess and I skipped brushing my teeth. I know I wore a clip-on tie that was not fully stuffed under my lapel. Still, I followed protocol and after the interview, sent a "thank you" letter. I thought it would be a novel idea to type it up on toilet paper, as Vicky and Kate seemed like cool people. It would give them something to talk about years down the road.

Four days later, I got a call from Vicky. She offered me a full-time job as a Vocational Retention Specialist, and not the part-time one I interviewed for. The position needed my level of education and paid $21,000 a year, with health and dental benefits.

"By the way," she added, "I laughed hysterically at the toilet paper letter. That's the kind of humor we need around here! Just don't do it again."

I half smiled, not knowing how to take that comment. I then asked Vicky if I could get back to her in a few days with a decision, and she stoically replied, "Ahh, yeah, I guess so."

This job offer caught me totally off guard. I was blind-sided. I had no idea what a Vocational Retention Specialist was. I didn't care what it paid, or if it offered any benefits. I was just ecstatic that I was finally offered a full-time job. Furthermore, I'd be using my degree! No one had EVER offered me employment to this magnitude!

But to me, this was more than just a full-time job offer. It was a statement. The message I heard from Vicky was, *"Steve Martell, you have the education and talent to offer a service that can help society - and we want it!"* Those were the most precious, unspoken words I ever heard. I never, *ever* imagined I would hear those words. I was swept back to when I was in a coma, and I thought I was dead. Now I was alive and experiencing a dream I didn't even know I could dream!

This job would propel me into society as a productive human being. It would mean I was an educated adult with a career. No longer am I a "disability." I envisioned puffing out my chest with some majestic voice announcing in the air: *"STEVEN MARTELL, M.S., C.R.C., REHABILITATION COUNSELOR!"* A big **"S"** would be stitched on my shirt, as my cape would flail in the wind.

After I got this offer, I yelled in glee so loud the whole town heard me! I called Mom first, of course, and told her. Then I called my siblings, friends from college, professors, Patricia at VESID, and my former band members. Most of them were at work and didn't answer, so I haphazardly called random numbers from the phone book.

I rang someone's phone, and a tin voice said," Hello?"

"I GOT THE JOB!" I exclaimed. "CAN YOU BELIEVE IT!?"

Pause…"Who is this?"

"Does not matter, BECAUSE I GOT IT!!"

"Freak."

CLICK!

I dialed another number.

RING!…**RING!**…

"Hello?"

"I GOT THE JOB!"

"Congratulations. What job?"

"I don't know, some retention job, ALL I KNOW IS I GOT IT!"

"Do I know you?"

"NO!"

CLICK

One more

RING!

"Croden's Meat Market, can I help you?"

"I GOT THE JOB!"

Pause… "Do you want to make an order? We have a special on pork bellies."

"NO PORK BELLIIES, *'CAUSE I GOT THE JOB!!'*"

"What are you on, kid?"

CLICK!

I didn't wait a few days to give my answer. I called Vicky back after less than an hour of jubilant celebration. Then, in a coy and sophisticated tone, I said, "I've decided that I would accept your offer." I couldn't believe I waited even a second to say "yes" and jeopardize Vicky rescinding this job offer.

On the Road to Work

As a law, a person with a disability cannot work full-time after that 9-month trial work period and still get SSD. I was apprehensive about working and losing those benefits, quite honestly. What if I lose my benefits because of working full-time then find out the doctors were right?? Then I'd have no money at all! I started looking more into the Social Security work incentives.

I found out there was more to it…*much more then I realized.* I exposed the 36-month re-entitlement Period. This meant that, if within 36 months of losing SSD due to work activity, if my income fell below the Substantial Gainful Activity amount, or I found out my disability did prevent me from working, my full benefits would be reinstated, *no questions asked!*

What a deal! Or… did I find bad information?

I thought this was too good to be true. I heard so many horror stories about working full-time while on Social Security, causing one to lose benefits and their job, and then living off cat food. I didn't want to become one of the "public benefit casualties." So, I met with a Social Security representative at the Syracuse office. I found out it was <u>exactly</u> what I researched. Knowing this gave me enough confidence to attempt full time employment, even though I'd have my SSD taken from me. I was finally in control of my own financial destiny.

The night before my first day at Supports Unlimited, I was up all night, as excited as a kid on Christmas Eve. At the same time, I was apprehensive about what my job would be, if I could retain the information to do it, if I could take notes with my right hand, or even if I could stay awake the entire day!

I headed into work the next morning. Kate did an orientation that first day and explained the job as a Vocational Retention Specialist. My job was to go to different job sites where people with mental or psychological disabilities were working and make certain they were doing their job okay. These people learned the basics of their job through job coaching via Supports Unlimited, then went out working on their own. If the worker or the employer had problems, I would intervene and try to help solve it with counseling or negotiating with their employer. If the clients couldn't do the job anymore or quit, the agreement was that I would temporarily do the job until there was a replacement. However, if it ever came down to me doing the job, then as a reasonable accommodation staff would help me out. I also provided encouragement to people with disabilities to continue working, often as a peer example.

Furthermore, my job duties included identifying, meeting, and helping people with disabilities in the Consolidated Industries Sheltered Workshop who I thought could work in the community. This position would involve me helping them to leave the workshop and becoming a productive working member of the community, to the degree of their capabilities. I was empowering people with disabilities who didn't realize they had the power to become active members of society. In a way, I was working with my younger self.

It wasn't that long ago that I felt like the outcast to society. I no longer have that perspective, and I had the chance to help others put that murky viewpoint in the past. *If I ever needed motivation to do the best darn job I could, this job WAS the motivation!*

I finally got my first paycheck; it was monumental one. I had my basic living costs covered, so I used that first check to get cable television installed for my mom. At the same time, she could see how much happier I was compared to past years. I could see how much happier she was seeing how I was happier. This "happiness" became reciprocal, and I didn't want it to stop!

But unfortunately, my mother's health was failing, and she had to go on kidney dialysis. She was a shut in; cable television was her only means of recreation. My gift helped fill her days and nights and gave her a new hobby. Television was now on 24 hours a day as compared to years past, when it would "sign off" to the National Anthem.

Adjusting To Work

I was now part of the handicapped community, which put me in a unique position to work with consumers with disabilities. The best part was that I wasn't afraid to admit being in this population. I mean, how many people could have a lobotomy, die, go to hell, then get better, only to send good vibrations to their peers? In a way, I found my place in life not only through my job, but in my own acceptance of myself. I used a mix of my humor, optimistic attitude, empathy, and motivation to send this message:

"Be proud of who you are and don't think you can only survive by being sheltered in an industrial warehouse. Instead, forge ahead as a citizen who contributes to the mechanics of the community and dive into life. Run on the wild side."

I wanted people to love themselves to allow the community to love them. Also, I could not be a friend to my consumers, as doing so could be a conflict of interest, but nothing stopped me from being *friendly.* I wanted to treat people with my own unique, holistic approach and not with a therapeutic attitude. I knew I was already at their peer level; I wanted to leverage our similarities and show them how to best help themselves.

I never wanted to be "textbook" in my repertoire of counseling skills, but I did come up with subtle techniques, such as reflecting feelings, paraphrasing and using unconditional positive regard. My aim was to always keep the professional relationship going so effective problem solving could be introduced. At the same time, I wanted to create a non-threatening relationship with me, the counselor. This foundation could help the consumers focus on themselves.

This full-time gig not only gave me the opportunity to develop and polish my counseling rapporteur, but it also allowed me to adjust my sleep time. I could gauge how much mental fatigue and stress I could take at work before needing a break to prevent myself from breaking. Working part-time gave me the flexibility to rest when not working. Now, I was going to try to perform eight hours straight. My number one setback was that my brain injury caused me to get tired faster than anyone else, so I had to figure out how I could keep pace with the able-bodied community.

I learned to go to bed earlier, get up earlier and *slowly* move through my exercises. Physically exhausting myself early wasn't an option. I didn't rush myself *mentally* at work either, because then I would run out of "energy" by the end of the day (i.e., get confused and lose concentration). I learned how to pace myself and set daily goals, prioritizing them so the least important tasks were saved for the end of the day. If I became too tired to reach some of those end-of-day goals, they could flow into the next day, because I already built wiggle room into my agenda. If by some wild chance I had my wiggle room free, I could always straighten my desk up.

Everyone knows life events suddenly occur, so my schedule had to be adjusted when the unexpected came up. That's when time management skills come into play. This is my own personal regiment that works for me; it may be different for others, so I never tell people to duplicate what I do. Instead, assess yourself and see what helps YOU reach your personal goals. Work within your own guidelines and established boundaries. What I want you to take from this is that you are capable of discovering those boundaries because you understand your disability better than anyone else, with paying respect to the doctors.

Pride in Doing It on My Own

It was inevitable that I would lose my SSD and have to live from my earnings. After taxes, my full-time job was only $200 more than what I earned on SSD, but you know what? It was my own money I earned. I was also starting to pay FICA taxes to build Social Security up for my retirement. I took the risk of losing my SSD benefits, and I wound up learning it was no risk at all! I feel like I won because I can support myself. And, no, the

Social Security Administration is not paying me to write these words, because I live this even now!

In the end, my unique counseling techniques produced quality work, and I got a raise! I received a certification in Industrial Relations from Cornell University as a trainer for Social Security Disability and Supplementary Security Income work incentives. I found myself training staff and helping Social Security recipients in Central New York. Because Social Security is such a boring subject, I mixed my humor in it to try and make it interesting, as well as using myself as an example of how work incentives work.

Let me echo that I *am not* using my personal situation as a template for everyone to follow, but rather encouraging you to create your own template. Use my situation as inspiration to build your best darn template possible!

Mom's Sick

In early January 1997, I was at work filling out Medicaid billing forms around 5:00pm when the pager clipped to my belt started vibrating. I rolled my eyes, wondering why someone paged me so late in the day. It displayed a familiar phone number, but I just could not place it. I figured it had to be a client. I didn't hesitate to return the call.

It was my sister Diane. She said in a very calm, soft tone, "Steve, now don't get worked up, but something went terribly wrong with Mom when she was having kidney dialysis."

My heart jumped up in my throat. "What?" I said, holding my breath.

Again, she was calm, "Her blood pressure suddenly dropped, and she had both a stroke and a heart attack at the same time." At this point her voice started trembling and I could tell she was holding back tears. "No one knows what is going to happen. Her temperature is uncontrollable. She's heavily medicated and her entire body is iced to bring her fever down."

I froze stiff, then frantically said, "What-what is she saying? Does she know what's going on? What are doctors saying??"

My sister sighed, "She fell into a coma. It doesn't look good."

At that point I turned pale. Diane told me what hospital and room number she was in. Ironically, it was the same hospital I was in 17 years prior.

For the next week I wept going back and forth to the hospital, always staying strong when around my mother. I usually joined my siblings at her bedside. As she laid motionless in her ice boat, I voiced words of encouragement to her. But could she hear them?

Everyone told me she felt no pain and couldn't hear, but I had my doubts. Flashes came back to me with vengeance. I remembered feeling nothing but pain and hearing those distant muffles. I remembered the screams, and the horror. Having been through this already, I felt that I could relate to her, and I prayed she wasn't going through what I had seen and felt.

One day I went up to the hospital to see my mother and no one else was there. I slowly walked into her room and looked up at the monitors. Different ones had blips, numbers, meters, and tics. I knew not what they meant, but I knew they worked in concert together to create an eerie scene that made time hold still. My mind started to remember that same scene when I was a patient in the same hospital.

I walked to her bedside and held her hand. I again quickly looked up to the monitors. They held the same numbers and created the same sounds. I looked back down to my mother's motionless body and gulped, trying to force a smile.

I said to her with a raspy voice, "Mom, it's Steve, your baby. They say you can't hear me, but I think you can. But if they're right and Heaven can tape record words, I hope they play these back to you some day." I gently rocked her hand, "Your baby is fine! I made it in life Mom, made it! I did it all without lawsuit money. We don't need no stinkin' lawsuit dollars! I did it with your love, compassion, and encouragement. Mom, I am going to take this further. You wait, you'll see. I'm taking this life you and Dad gave me and achieving things we never imagined! I have just begun to fight. I love you, Mom. You're my hero, my heart and soul. And you're going to get out of this hellish state you're in, I promise. One way or another, you will."

I kissed her forehead. My tears splashed on her face.

The next evening at 11:50pm, my phone rang at my apartment. It was my sister Patti, calling from the hospital. She softly said, "Steve, we lost Mom. I'm sitting next to her, holding her hand. She looks beautiful; in peace now."

I then stayed silent on the phone. There was no more need for words, as she just said it all. I thanked my sister for telling me and hung up the phone. That is when I stopped crying. *Our pain was gone.*

CHAPTER IX

REALITY...
AND REVENGE

It was now three weeks since my mother passed away, but I felt as if I still had something to prove to her. In a way, I felt like the car manufacture of my mangled car was responsible for her death. I believed they put unnecessary stress on her by winning my lawsuit and accelerated her demise. *Mom would be here today if it were not for them*, I selfishly thought, trying to blame the manufacturer for her death. It seemed like they felt pleasure in punishing her for even *thinking* of suing someone as great and powerful as **them**!

Now life started to get personal. Strange as it seems, I dreamt of avenging her death by living a life of extreme bliss. The automobile maker wanted to bring me to my knees while my mother watched helplessly. I wanted to be the happiest person in the world for my mother's sake, because they carelessly struck her dreams down and laughed while she was bleeding.

The best way I could avenge my mother's death was by being her vigilante, as I saw the auto maker's attorneys as the nemesis, the criminals. I had no idea how I was going to do this so I may have been giving myself false promises. My mother started my lawsuit and the car maker won, but somehow, I wanted her to get the last laugh. Somehow, some way.

· · ·

One day after working at Supports Unlimited, I was invited to an after-work get-together of various counselors, psychologists, and social workers. While there, Bill Woods, a well-known local rehabilitation counselor who was working at the Syracuse VA Medical Center, told me of an opening at the VA for a Vocational Rehabilitation Counselor and encouraged me to apply for it. He explained to me this job would be twofold, as half the time I would be administering vocational rehabilitation to patients of the Syracuse VA Hospital, and the other half I would be providing case management services to veterans with severe mental disabilities.

Although I was happy with the work I was doing and the population I served, this job would be an ultimate career position. Even the lowest salary it offered would be considerably more than what I was getting at the non-profit I worked at. Furthermore, the pay was almost double of what I would be getting with SSD!

My thoughts about getting the VA job were, *although I could not be a war hero like my father, at least I could help US Veterans who served this country.* The job was more clinical than what I was used to, but I was inclined to at least apply. *Why not?* I thought. *Getting this job would be a dream, but a long shot at best.* In my favor, I had both education and experience on my resume. So, I rolled up my sleeves and submitted my application.

About a week after my submission, I got a phone call while sitting in my office at work. It was Dan O'brien-Mazza, the Coordinator of VA Vocational Services, who said he is going to offer the job to either myself or another person he interviewed that morning. He went on to say, "I'm not going to interview you, as I pretty much know how you work. There is going to be a federal hiring freeze in about three weeks, so, who it is offered to hinges on who can start earlier, so I'm going to ask you both the same question: *if I was to offer you the job tomorrow, could you start in three weeks?* That would allow you to give your employer a two-week notice if you wish."

I crouched forward and whispered in the phone, "Yes, absolutely!"

"Okay then, I'll call you tomorrow and let you know either way," he said.

The conversation I just had did not seem real—I'm being considered for a federal job as a counselor! This would be a grand slam home run any person would drool over, let alone someone with multiple disabilities like me. Even if I did not get the offer, me being the first runner-up for a job in a government agency would be the makings for bragging rights.

About an hour later, my office phone rang. It was Dan again, and this time he said, "Steve, I'm not waiting until tomorrow, I would like to offer you the position of Vocational Rehabilitation Counselor, Grade 11; step one, starting at $38,560 annually. Would you accept?"

This was the ultimate surreal moment; I could not believe the words I was hearing.

"YESSIR!" I exclaimed, not caring who overheard me, and some heads did swing my way. He said I would get a conditional offer letter from HR later in the week and directions on the background check and drug screening. If all is clear, I'll get a starting date.

I hung up the phone and sat back and smiled, thinking to myself: *Steve Martell, severely disabled and can hardly walk, is the happiest person in the world. Even happier now than how happy I already was, as the good fortune just keeps piling on!!* I now could hear my mother laughing. She lost the battle, but she finally won the war.

. . .

I started the job at the Syracuse VA on a crisp day in December. The population I was to serve provided quite a challenge to me. They had an abundance of disabilities like Post Traumatic Stress Disorder, multiple contusions, and brain injuries. Also, there was a heavy slant to concurrent disabilities, often combat related or due to trauma.

As a vocational rehabilitation counselor, my job was to help Veterans with disabilities who were unemployed, underemployed, or unsuitably employed to secure community or federal jobs and careers. I was also a case manager under the supervision of Gary Kline, serving Veterans with severe mental illness and those going through psychological trauma.

I intertwined the dry humor I inherited from my father with curative counseling, which created a unique approach when addressing Veterans with disabilities. Much like my last job, my disability helped me broach diverse issues: I became a peer example. As I indicated earlier, a disability discriminates from no one, including United States Veterans. It just seems to hit home much more with them. American soldiers risk becoming people who are disabled by being in harm's way. If this happens, the least I could do is help them the best I could.

Additionally, I wanted to do soul searching as to what I have in common with Veterans. Suddenly, it became obvious— the answer was right under my nose: *I am a product of Veterans!* There is *no way* I could have done what I did in life had it not been for the foundation God and our Veterans created. When the military works together, may it be with security, protection, or combat, it becomes a well-oiled machine called the United States of America! I now felt closer to my father than ever. I started to understand his great contribution to the United States.

I decided I would approach this job three ways. First, when I conduct an orientation about our services for Veterans, I end it by telling them about me wanting to be a Marine like my father. I continue to explain how my plans were torn apart by my accident, and then being rehabilitated by multiple services this great nation has to offer which *they* protected. By volunteering this information, I start to create a footing for a strong working relationship.

Second, I wanted to create a relaxing and non-threatening office setting, much like my office in my previous job, but with an added slant. So, in my office I have a shadow box with my father's military picture and campaign metals in it, sports memorabilia, antique clock, positive soldier memorabilia scattered about, and a Billy Bass on the wall. In other words, I make my space a warm setting and closer to walking into a quiet home study than a clinical room.

A third counseling approach I would use is how I talked one-to-one with Veterans. I would use a light, cheerful attitude, but treat the Veterans with the respect and dignity they deserve. However, never would I make light of a Veteran in deep crisis, but rather employ encouragement and bridge them to the appropriate services. It's no secret that suicide ideation is high among Veterans, so I always took this subject seriously.

My counseling approach seemed to work wonderfully, based on the positive feedback I received from Veterans. Yes, I would use traditional counseling approaches like motivational interviewing, but I found the eclectic approach the best. This approach is customizing your counseling style depending on what works best with the client. It's not counseling by shooting from the hip but instead having multiple tools to use as situations evolve.

As time passed, I refined my counseling approach. The more I collaborated with Veterans, the more counseling tools I would develop. I would solidify more relationships with community resources. I polished my repertoire of intervention abilities.

The beauty behind this job is my counseling was not court mandated, as people came to me for help on a voluntary basis. If it was court mandated, some people may knock on my door just to please their parole officer. This is important because I did not have to force myself to help people that didn't want to be helped.

In a way I started to get cocky with my abilities, now having access to multiple means to help *any* person with a disability, not just Veterans. There was a swagger to my walk, and I saw myself as the premiere counselor. I thought I had all the resources and knew how to use them to improve the world. However, Norm Mattice brought me down to earth.

Bursting My Balloon

Norm still wandered around homeless, collecting cans and never turning down change from a pedestrian or motorist. I helped him out the best I could but learned not to give him cash for groceries, as it would go directly to booze. So, me buying Norm gift cards to fast-food restaurants became his mainstay for nutrition, assuming he didn't get a sandwich at the Rescue Mission first. Elliott also lent a hand the best he could but was as confused as me at his cousin's resistance.

I offered to get Norm situated with psychiatric care, as I previously helped him get Medicaid and he could pay a psychiatrist with this health benefit. He did not see himself as having a mental illness, although his bizarre actions were far beyond the norm of society. I tried to get him hooked-up with state vocational rehabilitation, but he felt as if he had no disability. I tried to get him qualified for transitional housing, but he did not want to live in a group home. I was doing what I never wanted to do and was *forcing* help on Norm. It became an obsession! EVERY public service I tried to get him situated with he declined. I got to the point that I would yell at him then *plead* that he'd take my bait. He just snubbed my efforts.

Norm once said to me, "You only know about federal programs." He then stood to attention and said like a robot, "My name is Steve Martell, and I know everything and can rescue you from yourself." Norm would not listen to reason from me or his family, even his favorite Aunt Carol.

A week later, Norm was found dead under a wooden ramp in a town next to Syracuse. An empty bottle of vodka was found next to his head. The official cause of death was hypothermia, accelerated by alcohol consumption. Seeing how he had no family, and his parents were deceased, Maura Kennedy, a singer and songwriter, made a Gofundme account to generate money for his wake. I partnered with her and as a result, Norm had a king's funeral. In fact, we had left over cash we donated to organizations we know Norm appreciated.

I remember coming home after Norm's calling hours and laying down on my sofa, a tear running down my face. All the fun times we shared and the dreams we had where now shattered. *How did I go wrong?* I thought. *With all the counseling knowledge I have, and all of the community resources I have at my fingertips, I could not help my childhood best friend.*

Then reality hit me: much like a person who is court man-dated for counseling, Norm fell into the population I did not know how to work with. It's actually people no one can work with. *It's the population who do not want to help themselves.* But Norm was dead-spot-on with his sarcasm: I *don't* know every-thing, and I *can't* save everyone. His death humbled me and made me reevaluate the part of human services I was ignorant about. I was setting my competencies too high and trying to help people with tools only God has.

Adjusting Personal Needs

As I got older and started to advance my career, some phys-ical disabilities I had increased. Furthermore, some new ones developed. This was no surprise, but I was still determined to make things work. I had to modify my physical therapy routine, which still involved stretching out muscles on my paralyzed side. But now I would do this so my working muscles would move my paralyzed ones and pull them like they're almost working. Also, as a reasonable accommodation, I worked on a compressed schedule, which saw me work 9-hour days, but I got every other Friday off. I just had to readjust pacing my day. This extra day off gave my body some quality time to rejuve-nate, much like consolidating class hours at Columbia College or having a "bye" week in the NFL.

My career at the VA was truly in full swing, thanks to Norm for my reality check. I felt extremely comfortable working with anyone who had a significant problem. Over the years my job faded from case management, allowing me to dedicate much of my time to psychosocial counseling. My career long colleague, Kathy, provided vocational rehabilitation therapy. I provided rehabilitation counseling and developed work incentive programs for Veterans. Ernie provided peer support. Shelley led our unit and provided guidance. Lisa ran our supported employment program. Other team members came and left. We became a well molded team and took pride in enriching the lives of Veterans!

Besides my work with veterans, I now developed and presented community presentations. These presentations involved PowerPoint shows, sometimes with several pictures of me before, during and after my car accident, and my rocky but steady climb through rehabilitation. Also, other presentations I developed to educate people were how to use Social Security Work Incentives and the different types of Veteran benefits. I used myself as a real-life example and almost everything I presented I experienced, so basically I became my own "cheat-sheet".

I would customize my presentations to directly hit the heart of the population I presented to. This was not only to people with disabilities for motivation, but also mental and physical health students. My presentations blossomed to state and community colleges, public forums and even clergy gatherings. I spoke to large audiences, like at Caesar's Palace, where I talked of pitfalls and victories of pursuing higher education with a severe brain injury. I was the keynote speaker at a graduation ceremony for SUNY Upstate College of Health Professionals. I was driven to make health professionals be proud of what they were doing, and at the same time thanking them for helping people with disabilities, like me.

However, there was one common rule with every presentation I did for anyone: it had to involve inspiration and end on a positive note. *That was a must, and I would have it no other way!* I would not "sugarcoat" the message but leave it open ended for a path to a brighter future.

One time I was at home putting together one of my presentations in my mancave, when I started to get fatigued. *Pace yourself,* I thought to myself, so I sat back and took a breather. Suddenly, a text came on my cell phone that I did not recognize.

It read: "PayPal member. We have found some potentially fraudulent activity on your PayPal account. Please call 048-***-**** to speak to a PayPal official."

I smiled and nodded my head. To me, that text was a gift from above. I was curious to learn what all the noise was about, especially knowing I didn't have a PayPal account.

I called the phone number, and a woman with broken English answered, "Hello, this is Cindy from PayPal Detection Services, who am I speaking to today?"

I said, "This is Fred, Fred Delleco."

"Yes, how are you today Mr. Delleco? I would like to inform you that we found some unusual activity on your PayPal account."

I said in a startled tone, "No way, how could this be? Cindy, please help me, what do I do?"

Cindy said, "Well, let me ask you a question: *have you used your PayPal account in the last 14 days?*"

I thought for a second, "Hummm, I don't think so. Why?"

"Oh dear," she said. "I was afraid of that. Because $412.14 was extracted from it by Rayceeme.com Adult Store. Another $250.00 is scheduled to come out next month."

I thought for a second, "Oh yeah, I forgot, that was me."

"What?" Cindy said, a bit startled. "You made that purchase? Are you sure? Because if you don't put a stop to that activity, another $250.00 will come out in two weeks. And there is no telling what will come out in the future."

"Don't put a stop to it," I pleaded. "I've been waiting for that to come! It's for a state-of-the-art silicone doll, called 'Screaming Candy.' I hope it's delivered in a secured box, so the dogs don't get to it."

"But Mr. Delleco..."

"It's really cool. You squeeze the breast, and it makes yummy sounds. The hair is optional."

"This is crazy," Cindy said, then hung the phone up.

I grinned and ended the call. My breaktime was a short one, but a fruitful one. Norm would have been proud.

CHAPTER X

WHERE WE'VE BEEN & WHERE WE'RE GOING

In March of 2002, I attended a surprise fiftieth birthday party for my sister Patti at a local banquet hall. After she turned the corner and people surprised her at this gala event, light music rang out and the hors d'oeuvres tables were open for business.

At one of the buffet tables, I was trying to pour myself a drink of soda from a flimsy, 2-liter plastic bottle, when a woman standing at the same table saw me struggling to tip it.

"Excuse me," she said. "Do you need help?"

I smiled, "No thank you, I got it." At that point, my limp hand slipped off the bottle and it crashed onto the table. I caught the plastic bottle just before it toppled over; the woman rushed over and helped me stand it upright.

"You sure?" she said, as we both embraced the bottle with our hands. I released my grip and stepped back.

"Tell you what," I said, bowing my head. "I would be honored if you would pour me a drink."

She smiled, "I know you could do it yourself, it's just that I'd hate to see this nice, white tablecloth be stained with black cherry soda."

I chuckled a bit and observed her as she filled my cup. While studying her, I couldn't but notice she looked familiar. I could have sworn I saw her before. But for the life of me, I couldn't remember when or where, or if it were something I just imagined.

She handed me the drink, "Thank you," I said. "And I'm sure the janitor is thankful, as well."

"Janitor?" she said.

I took a swig of soda. "Yeah," I said, wiping my mouth with my sleeve, "no mess to mop up on the floor."

The woman smiled again. "You want a napkin?"

"Too late now. My shirt sleeve just took the brunt of my slobber." I paused and studied her for a second more, "You look familiar. Do I know you from somewhere? "

"I just jumped out and yelled 'surprise' to Patt," she said grinning. "Maybe that's how you know me. Say, how do you know Patt anyway?"

As the woman talked, I lazily flopped back in a chair at a nearby empty table. "Sorry, I must sit down before I fall down." The woman followed my lead and sat next to me. "How do I know her?" I asked. "She's my sister."

"Really?" said the woman. "We both work together. I'm also a nurse, like Patt." On the table in front of her was an abandoned invitation to someone for the surprise party. It had a picture of my sister on it, with her married and maiden names in gold print. The woman looked at it and read it aloud: *"Patti (Martell) Briest"*.

The woman looked up, "You're Steve Martell?"

"Yes," I said with a surprised look. "How did you know?"

"You were in some band and played at my school when I was a kid!" she said with a gleam. "My name is Mari Grace Ludlow, at least it was before I got divorced."

I fell into deep thought, trying to think back twenty years ago. *Mari Grace*, I thought. Then, a foggy image of her at a gig we had at Miller Hawk Jr. High came back. I also faintly remember Norm and Dan talk about her having a muscle builder boyfriend.

I asked, "Your mother is Rose, right? Used to be a hall monitor? And didn't you used to date some strong guy?"

Mari Grace rolled her eyes, "Yes. Didn't work out. He wanted me to be a housewife. Be pregnant and in slippers, with dinner on the table when he came back from work. Those events were NOT going to happen!"

"Huh," I said, "if I was married, wouldn't care if she cooks and I'd HELP her get a job! Hell, I'd eat SpaghettiOs' out of a tin can, as long as she works."

Everything about Mari Grace gradually came back to me. I remember her watching me as I played drums at her Jr. high dance. I got bold. "Say, I got a question for you. Why were you looking at me so much at that dance at the Jr. high? You know, twenty years ago?"

"Was I?" She spoke. "Do you want me to lie or tell you the truth?"

"I...don't know how to answer that." I perked up, "Tell you what, let the truth be known. Give it to me straight."

"Okay," Mari Grace said. She then leaned forward and hypnotized me with her eyes, "Because I thought your band sucked!"

"What?" I said, secretly mortified. "Sucked?"

She nodded her head, "Yep, sucked. Oh, by the way, I always wondered, why did you stop playing drums on 'Do you Wanna Dance'?"

I frowned again, "Because that was the end of the song, and the other guys mistakenly went on playing."

"Oh," she said. "Yep, I thought you were a bad band. Besides, I got to admit, I wanted to look at you: a cute but jerky, irresponsible, loudmouth punk rocker who used to wear a fake leather jacket he bought at K-mart."

I finally defended myself; retaliation was in order: "Interesting, because I saw you as a stuck-up, prissy princess who thought her shit didn't stink!"

Mari Grace and I then became silent and stared at each other. Suddenly, without notice and with no cue, we both started busting out laughing.

I said in tears of hysterics, "So, are you still prancing around in slippers and popping out babies?"

She quickly shot back, "Do you still wear that blue light special fake leather jacket?"

I shook my head, "Naa, they had to cut it off from me when I got into a car accident."

Mari Grace started to become serious. "I remember hearing about that. Patt told me she had a brother who got into a car accident. How are things now?"

I shrugged my shoulders, "Eh, I can't complain. Besides being disabled for life, I pull my own weight. I graduated from S.U. with a couple of master's degrees and I'm a counselor at the VA." I nodded my head, "Life is good Mari, life is good."

"Amazing," said Mari Grace with a dead pan expression, shaking her head. "Just amazing. I remember reading about you in the paper. Look how far you've come."

I then looked down and said with a shy, western draw, "Aww, shoot Miss Mari, ain't 'nuting a 'lil cowhand couldn't do!"

Mari reached over and grabbed my arm, "No, seriously Steve, what you have done with your life is amazing! People could learn a lot from you. You should write a book someday to inspire other people in similar circumstances. Heck, you inspire me!"

Mari and I left the party separately, but later that evening we met at her apartment and reminisced about old days, filing through old yearbooks while laughing about past friends and teachers. Also, we discovered we had similar values, including human service jobs and personal life goals.

Mari Grace and I phoned each other daily for about a week, which morphed into dating each other. I felt carefree and relaxed around her, and my heart fluttered with her every kiss. I don't know how she felt about me but based on the fact she always wanted me by her side, I think our thoughts were similar.

Another thing we had in common was our humor. We almost had telepathic minds and could play off each other. Mari Grace would often smile at me when she knew what I was thinking.

Once we went out to dinner and the waitress introduced herself to us. The waitress saw I had physical problems, which she must have thought translated to being mentally challenged. She asked Mari Grace what she wanted to drink. After taking her order the waitress gestured to me.

"What will he have?" she asked.

Mari Grace turned to me, "What do you want to drink?" she asked.

While looking at the menu I said, clearly audible, "Tell her I want a Bud Light."

Nodding her head, she turned to the waitress, "He said he wants a Bud Light."

The waitress turned red; the people sitting next to us almost wet their pants.

I was proud to call Mari Grace my girlfriend. She also became my best friend. Who could ask for anything more? However, although I was full of self-confidence, still my heart was a bit cautious. Mari Grace was a beautiful, totally able-bodied woman. Why would she want to date a guy like me when she could have any guy she wants?

Once I was shopping in a mall with Mari Grace when I got tired walking and had to sit on a bench. Mari got me a coffee and herself an iced tea from a side vendor, then sat next to me.

After twenty seconds of silence, I said to her, "You know, we been seeing each other for, what, three months now, and—"

"Three months and two weeks," she shot in.

"And two weeks, right." I grinned, then looked directly in her aqua eyes. "How do you feel going out with a badly disabled guy?"

Mari Grace then smiled. "I don't see a disabled guy. I see the love of my life." She leaned forward and kissed me.

Eventually, in a small ceremony with Pastor Bob officiating, we were married in front of our families. Suddenly, I was a family head, with stepchildren, in-laws, and dogs of my own. My stepson Nicholas was in the US Navy and got me a shirt that read, "Navy Dad." This made me happy. We bought a "fix-er-upper" brick home on a country hill, and we settled down. New Life Temple of Praise church became our second home, run by Bishop Dewberry and his wife, Pastor Cindy. I was proud to have Mari Grace take my last name.

-Oh, and Hazel's prophecy that no one could ever love me was debunked-

• • •

After Mari and I were happily married about 10 years, Hazel and I ran into each other in a local grocery store. We were both free, so decided to go to the corner café for coffee. I had not sat down and talked with her face-to-face in the thirty-three years since she left me, so this was rather uncomfortable. However, I felt as if I had to follow-up with it. For some strange reason I think she felt the same way.

After we talked about our personal lives over the past several years, she said with a somber expression, "Steve, I'm sorry." Her eyes started to well up.

Me, knowing exactly what she meant, quickly said, "Hazel, we were kids. No apology needed."

She shook her head and said, "I acted like a jerk," then dropped her eyes.

I reached across the table, held her right hand, and said, "No Hazel, no. You got it all wrong." Hazel raised her head and stared at me. "At the deepest, darkest time when I didn't know what reality or a lie was, life or death was, heaven or hell, outside of my family, you were there. No other person but you. Do you know much I looked forward to those phone calls from you when I was alone in the hospital? They kept me going and made an unbearable situation bearable. The love for you and what you did for my life, I could never even explain. You were the one bright light in my life to let me know that I was still human being. You provided the 'normalcy' in my life in my otherwise chaotic world."

I paused, then gently rocked her hand, "You pointed out a big fault in my life that I could never understand or see: *I've got to love myself before I can love anyone else.* You were the only person to have the guts to address it. And by saying what you said, you not only released yourself to grow, but you released me to grow."

Hazel's red eyes started tearing; a faint smile came over her. She got up from her plastic chair, walked around the table, and hugged me.

The Closure

After my meeting with Hazel, I drove home, climbed out of my dented SUV, and shut the door. I leaned on the vehicle a second and realized I just did something I never thought I'd do: I just forgave the person who trashed and scarred me for life. But that moment was more than just forgiving her. I just got plastic surgery on that scar! By pardoning and thanking her, I released almost thirty years of my pent-up insecurity. True, I already felt 99% better about myself, but there was 1% of unfinished business until now. I bent my head down and shook it in disbelief, all while smirking. I then gained my composure and walked into my home.

I tossed my car keys on a table and crashed into a recliner next to it. I reclined the chair back. It was quiet in the house, just the soft snore from my cat and a faint tic of the clock. This surreal moment with Hazel caused me to reflect on tragedies in my life. I started to have flashbacks, like my life coming to a screeching halt because of my car accident. Spending the next month "awake" during a coma, and convinced I was dead in hell. The realization I'll be disabled for life and hiding my head in the sand. And lastly, the stigma of having a brain injury and doctor's indirectly saying, "You got to beware."

But then my dark thoughts did a 360. I started thinking, *some people don't look at the "good" in their lives. They don't see the fun.*

I rationalized that a lead story on the evening news is always about the tragic event that happened to someone or some people. You never hear a lead story that Susan "Anyname" had a bouncing, 7-pound baby boy. Let's face it, tragedy sells and caters to the murky side of humans.

"You been crippled most your life," a person might say. *"Your life can't possibly be good!"*

Oh, contraire, my friends! Check this out: I can't but laugh thinking my father's pyramid really sharpened blades. I still can see the cross-eyed vision of a crayfish dangling from my nose. I scowled at my father for spanking me for swearing but loved him for teaching me respect. I can't forget Dave pushing my bicycle down a hill then me being swallowed by a hungry swamp willow. I remember whacking the T.V. set to stop it from rolling, and standing by it because the tube said, "Please stand by."

You know, it seems like yesterday that I feasted on carp and ants. I can still see my band having its inaugural practice session in a corn field. I thought it was hysterical seeing that kid in my review mirror, chasing my truck as I drove blind. I'll never forget stretching out on a bathroom floor at Arise and seeing high heels under the stall. I treasured the ecstasy of passing a college class, and invited the lessons learned by my failures. To this day I find enjoyment from robocalls. And, finally, nothing brings back memories like a good old chug of a cold Yoohoo.

I could go on and on about the rich days that molded me, and they still do! They far outweigh my dirty laundry. Yes, they keep shaping me, and well after becoming a person with a disability, too. But my point is it's easy to focus on the bad or tragic aspects of living, but too often the lush specks of life are never celebrated. They're swept under the rug. So, where does this leave you? It leaves despair and heartache on the carpet for you to see, while the features that enrich your life remain unnoticed.

I suggest when you're in an awkward position that irritates the bejesus out of you, put that event in your "life enrichment vault." When in life you're sad, lonely, and discouraged, open that vault up, expose those snippets. I guarantee those awkward events will have you shake your head and smile at the same time. Pay attention to the dragonflies of life, they follow you; they talk to you.

Don't get me wrong; I am not saying you should live in the past. I *never* would have gotten where I am had I remained stuck on memories. I'm saying you should march toward the future! But recalling a prolific past sets the foundation for achieving goals. A plush history advances a direction for your journey, and don't forget it!

Allow me to go back to that rug I talked about earlier. You know, where the specks of life are swept under it. I say, lift up that rug to expose those gems! Like I said at the start of this book, I hope you give yourself a chance. Remember, it took a lot of up's and down's, failures, victories, and heartaches, but I still gave myself a chance. And boy, I'm sure glad I did!

Did I ever want to toss in the towel? Hell yeah, and I would be a liar if I said I never did! How many times did I sit in class by the door, looking for a quick escape? Sometimes I would spend hours studying ducks when I should be in school. But the key is I always came back. Perhaps it took time, but I would circle around to my dream. Give it another shot. Take that placement test a second time and learn from my mistakes.

But at the same time, I knew when to say "when." I have been encouraged to get my PhD in Psychology. Could I do it? Perhaps. Would I be happy with it? Again, perhaps. Would I be happy with myself? Absolutely not. And why? Because I am too mentally tired to return to college. I find contentment with what I have. So, perhaps the doctors were right, maybe I shouldn't have exercised my brain. But their predictions were off just three degrees: associates, bachelors, and masters. The fact is I actually took their advice and didn't do calisthenics with my brain; instead, I exercised my heart. They never told me about that part.

I never went against medical advice, and never will! I don't want to give people the impression I'm saying to rebel against all clinicians or have a revolution against science. When they said to take it slow, I did. I took caution in every attempt I made and calculated every step I crafted. I left out a key part in this book: all during my journey I saw neurologists, physical therapists, and other various clinicians. I still do. Without listening to them I don't know where I would be. But I know I wouldn't be writing this book, I'll tell you that much!

My experiences caused me to reflect more about relationships. When someone abandons you that you trust your whole heart with, it's easy to cave in. Check out my obsession with Hazel. When she left me, I became suicidal, feeling as if she took my heart when leaving me. Her disturbing words that "no one could ever love you" became a mainstay with me for years. But you know, she never really took my heart. No, but what she did though was expose my dependent insecurities that I *thought* were my heart. In other words, I confused love with my irrational compulsion. Not good.

I can officially sum myself up into one phrase: *I am the happiest person alive!* I'm sure my mother knows. And why am I the happiest person alive? Simply because I didn't play victim to my hell and wanted to crawl out of that putrid valley. I can't believe I'm going to type these next few words, but I'm kind of glad for the wisdom I got from my disablement. Am I happy I'm a person with a disability? Hell no-I'm brain injured, not crazy! I'd much rather learn life lessons while being able bodied—playing the drums, hiking down a trail, or jogging around the house. But, as Mrs. Ross would say, "I guess that wasn't in God's plans."

I must mention that some may think I'm saying the only route to being the happiest person alive is by going to college. This is far from the truth. Keep this in mind: *college is not for everyone!* All disabilities come with their own unique circumstances. I know some people with brain injuries who can't stay awake very long or their attention span is only a few hours. That's the nature of their personal "hell." But I believe we people with disabilities claim victory by reaching our highest potential with what we have to work with; we should not gauge it against someone else's achievements. I'm not talking about a "participation trophy" here, I'm talking about earning your stripes!

So then, what is going to college? I'll tell you what it is, it's simply a tool to help reach your goals. If you have a disability that precludes higher education, then your goal may be independent living, like shopping, expressing yourself with artwork, getting a strike at that bowling lane, or maybe volunteering at your local shelter to serve food to the homeless. You think that feeding the homeless is not reaching a goal? Well, let me tell you this, brothers and sisters, go ask that destitute person if they didn't appreciate you serving them a hot meal.

Here's another goal: make a club! In the early 1980's my brother-in-law Larry and two other guys started to go deer hunting the same weekend every year. They jokingly called themselves the Swinedogs, and that annual weekend they would rent out a lodge in the wilderness. Larry invited me to go once.

I would not hunt, but I would stay back and enjoy nature while they would search for game.

That weekend allowed me to decompress from worries and issues in my life, most notably the Hazel debacle. I suggested we turn it into a club. Thus, Swinedog Training Camp was born. As of this day the club is now over fifteen people and even dipping into generations!

How did this all start? It started by my suggestion of forming a club and then working with a team to fine tune it, year after year. The club is not only fun, but the camaraderie formed in it makes life a bit more enjoyable!

My point in making: *a goal could be forging and crafting something, even an idea, then maintaining and enriching it for years to come!* A goal does not have to be a "one and done" event. Think around the circle. I bet you could think of a thousand other revolving goals I never even dreamt of!

Getting Close to the Finish Line

In spring of 2018 I conducted a PowerPoint presentation to about fifty people with disabilities, both acquired handicaps and ones born with disabilities. I sat in a chair in the middle of a stage and took them through my life journey of highs and lows, with humor and sincerity, but always underscoring inspiration.

At the end of it I paused with a taut silence, then continued. I felt inclined to curve my presentation into philosophy. It had been two years to the very day they found Norm's body, when I gave this speech. He was in back of my mind as I spoke:

"I guess humankind has many 'valleys of hell' to navigate around," I announced. "Yeah, these valleys are not just secluded to people having a disability like me, but to whatever life circumstances play out. You know, like a disheveled, homeless person, inclined to collect change…a person addicted to drugs…a person who was abused…one in jail…a sickly person, and the list goes on and on."

I sipped some water and continued, "I believe in any of life's trials a person can do one of two things: surrender to their hell or use that hell as a springboard. If you use a springboard approach, you have the potential to move mountains. But if you fall victim to the hell, then you're going to implode. And it's going to kill you, it's going to kill you really good. Why? Because you're going to identify with your hell and always swim in that cesspool."

I smiled and raised my right pointer, "The secret is to size up your personal hell, take note of where you want to be in life, then take the correct steps to climb out of that hell. You gotta have faith, as my father taught me."

At that point, I looked to my right, and recoiled my head like I was addressing someone else, "Steve, are you crazy?" I said with a scowl. "You hit your head or 'sumptin?" The crowd made a low mumble of laughter, "You make it sound so simple!"

I looked back to the audience, returning to my lecture, "No, it's not simple. As-a-matter of-fact, one of the hardest things in life is to save your own life."

I leaned forward in my chair and grasped my hands together, "Check this out: prove that hell wrong and celebrate the little victories that squelched it. The hell may be a class you didn't take, but the victory is checking off the class you passed. The hell may be someone saying no-one will ever love you, but the victory is when someone does. The hell can be the instruments not in sync, but the victory is when the band plays together. And, last but not least, the hell is being in a coma, but the victory is living when you're out. This is my personal philosophy and I use it every day for everything…and because of it I'm the happiest person in the world!"

"Now," I said quickly, tossing my shoulders back. "I'm not ignorant! There are events in everyone's life that aren't happy, ones that make you cry. They can be soldered in your memory for a lifetime. I had to watch my old bass player Eric take his last breaths from cancer and my 4-year-old grandson wither away from leukemia. My childhood friend drank himself to death. But I'm talking about being content with your continuum, no one is asking you to ignore the tragedy. Hey, isn't life a continuum with hiccups along the way?"

I smiled and arched my back, making an inviting gesture with my right hand, "C'mon people and join me at being the happiest person in the world!"

I then sat back with a smile and raised a fist, "…then rock on!"

One Final Word

So now here it is, January 11, 2020, and Mari and I are relaxing at home. I'm sitting at my desk typing this book with one fingernail on one finger, while she is playing with our three dogs on the living room floor. Our cat is observing the horseplay high on top the sofa. The fireplace is roaring, and my mother's sauce recipe is simmering in the crockpot. A lake-effect snowstorm is whipping-up outside.

On my desk is a small television set, where the Vikings and 49ers play an NFC divisional round. There is a cup of steamy Joe and a crushed can of Yoohoo to my right, and a computer in front of me. Everything in my life is hunky-dory; this is a 2020 Norman Rockwell still of the "American Dream."

I'm now coming down the stretch to retirement, and well-deserved retirement at that. Perhaps I'll pick up a second career; maybe I'll become a writer! I guess you will know I made this goal if you are reading these words. If you're not, I'll pursue something else, some other goal(s). Like, the grass must be mowed, rug vacuumed, and bathroom cleaned, before our dinner guests come over. My childhood friends Enid and Amy don't want to see a cluttered house! Mari has the full "honey-to-do" list; I'll check in with her later. She always says the man of the house makes all the important decisions, but the woman decides what's important.

Here's a surprise! As I type this, my cell phone is ringing! The phone's I.D. reads it's a caller from Owego, New York. I don't know anyone from Owego, but I sure do want a new friend from that town! So, I'm going to answer it:

"Hello," I say, in my most pleasant tone.

After the patented *blip* sound, native to most automated calls, a flat, robotic voice announces:

"This message is from the Bureau of Law Enforcement Services. There has been some illegal activity associated with your Social Security number. This could result in your immediate arrest and prosecution unless it is cleared up now. Press '1' now, to speak to one of our deputy experts. Press '1' now."

Needless to say, I was alarmed! I didn't hesitate to press "1". After listening to some pretty, digital cords, a foreign voice came on the phone, with a party of gibberish in the background.

"Hello, my name is Patrick, can I help you?"

"I hope you can," I said, "I got a message from someone saying I may be arrested? I have NEVER done anything wrong since I stole that candy bar when I was seven!" I then got more hectic, "Patty, you got to believe me!! Check out my background, I'm clean! I'm innocent! I used to be an altar boy and a Cub Scout leader!"

"Just calm down," Patrick said. "If you have not done anything wrong, then you need not worry. But it must be cleared up immediately. What is your name?"

"Ah, Fredrick, Fred Delleco. Will I be arrested??"

"Mr. Delleco, I can't say what actions law enforcement would take. My job is to clear this up before a warrant is issued for your arrest. Could you please tell me your Social Security number, so I can verify your identity?"

"Absolutely!" On my desk was an expired Lotto ticket. I read him the first nine numbers on it. "Would they put handcuffs on me if I'm arrested?"

"Possibly." Patrick was apparently putting my Lotto numbers in his computer, "Mr. Delleco, could you please repeat it, slower?"

I ignored him and calmed down, "Really? Handcuffs? I never been in handcuffs before. I can only imagine being vulnerable to anyone else's actions. It must be...*terrible!*"

"Yes Mr. Delleco, please repeat your..."

"They could do anything to me, and I would have no power, no say in the matter. Put an apple in my mouth, make me lick their boots, spank me. The possibilities are endless!"

I knew Patrick was getting irritated, "Mr. Delleco, this is a very serious matter."

"Kind of exciting if you should ask me. I think I saw this in 'Fifty Shades of Gray' before."

He made believe I was not talking, "Mr. Delleco, have you traveled out of the country in the last two years?"

"What, my country or your country? By the way, will you personally handcuff me?"

"Mr. Delleco - "

I said in a wimpy, sing-song voice, "Ohh, I been such a bad boy. I deserve to be spanked! But please, be gentle: I cry when I get horseradish in my sores."

That last comment was a success; it drew out expletives and a hang-up. I just sat back in my chair, put both arms behind my neck, then smiled.

-Yep, life sure is fun again! -

CONTACTS

To contact Steve or to have him speak at
your next function, email him at:

mari@steeringblind.com

• • •

Independent living

Independent Living Research Utilization (ILRU) creates
opportunities for independence for people with disabilities
through research, education, and consultation. You can also
locate independent living centers close to you. Check it out at:

https://www.ilru.org/

• • •

Social Security Administration (SSA)

If you receive Social Security benefits and want to learn more
about Social Security Work Incentives, check out:

https://www.ssa.gov/

• • •

Suicide Prevention Lifeline

If you are suicidal or in a crisis, dial the
Suicide Prevention Lifeline, at:

988

ABOUT THE AUTHORS

Steve Martell

Steve Martell (aka "Hunkey") resides in the snowy, upper hills of Syracuse, New York with his lovely wife, three dogs, cat, and Chia Pet. He has two successful stepchildren and two grandchildren, all who are his pride and joy. Steve has a plethora of contentment in life and credits God for everything he has. He proclaims that, despite becoming severely disabled, he is the happiest person in the world!

Hunkey never considered being a writer and author. Actually, writing was the furthest thing in his mind. He muses that the only creative writing he ever did was scribbling poems on a bathroom wall, and he read just three books in his life. Two of those books were forced on him by his 10th grade English teacher, and a third was Green Eggs and Ham. However, Steve has a story to tell, so he picked up his pen and started reflecting on his past.

• • •

Rebecca Mayglothling

Rebecca Mayglothing is an author and mother in Central New York. She has written hundreds of articles and ghost written five books. She enjoys hiking and watching horror movies with her Chihuahua.